I0199746

Historic Tales
— *of* —
LONG ISLAND CITY

GREATER ASTORIA HISTORICAL SOCIETY

THE
History
PRESS

Published by The History Press
Charleston, SC
www.historypress.com

Front cover, bottom: Long Island City waterfront (2020). *Shunsuke Takino Photography*.

First published 2022

ISBN 978-1-5402-5247-0

Library of Congress Control Number: 2022933373

This book is dedicated to the memory of

John Hart of Maspeth Kills (circa 1595–1668)
and May Svab (1898–1983), who lived in a Mathews Flat,

Who lived generations apart
Yet instilled in their families a deep love and respect for their community.

CONTENTS

ACKNOWLEDGEMENTS
AND NOTE ON SOURCES

*T*here are many whose work went into making this possible. Some people shared their family stories with us, and others shared fascinating tidbits from research they were doing, while others shared their talents.

Thank you to the Board of the Greater Astoria Historical Society, past and current, which has helped in many ways.

We have been blessed with a corps of extraordinary interns who assisted on many research projects and helped with our collections: Vernel Black, Marie Kessel, Susan Rahyab, Damian Silva, Ishraq Huda, Muhtady Shammo and Moinik Das. Thank you to the many other interns who were with us over summers past.

History is the story of people, shared and passed down to a new generation. We are grateful for the following people who contributed such amazing accounts with us:

- Great-grandson Steven Morgan of Patrick Jerome "Battle Axe" Gleason, the last mayor of Long Island City (chapter 31).
- Nephew Milton Mathews and other members of the Mathews family for information on Gustave X. Mathews (chapter 37).
- The late Alan Baum, whose father was a key employee of the Brewster Automobile Company (chapter 41).
- The late Paul Maringelli and the Bix Beiderbecke Sunnyside Memorial Committee (chapter 47).

- Grandson Jack Tissot for information on Emile E. Tissot (chapter 50).
- Nancy Ruhling, author of "Astoria Characters," March 10, 2010; reprinted with the kind permission of Nancy Ruhling's AstoriaCharacters.com (chapter 60).
- The stories shared with the historical society by Frank Carrado, the last "mayor of Long Island" (chapter 65).
- Research credit: Susan Rahyab (chapter 10).

Although there are many reference sources for this book gleaned from the Greater Astoria Historical Society library and other sources, the generosity of three people must be told.

William Quinn started and sustained the Greater Astoria Historical Society in its early years. The organization is his legacy to our community.

Charles Fertitta, of Creative Structures, a design firm, purchased the building that housed the former *Long Island Star-Journal*, a newspaper that was the "newspaper of record" for most of the Borough of Queens. When he started to clean out the building's basement, he discovered the newspaper's three-hundred-volume "morgue" (a popular term in the newspaper business to describe the file that holds past issues, or flats, held for reference purposes), which covered about half of the paper's print run that spanned the decades between the 1870s and 1960s. He donated them to the society, and we have used this invaluable narrative of our community's past to write a series of historical columns in the local press.

The third source is the late Vincent Seyfried, the "dean of the Queens County historians," who has written extensively on the Borough of Queens and donated a considerable portion of his archives to our society. To honor his generosity, our board has dubbed our library the Vincent Seyfried Research Center.

A special acknowledgment to the late Henry Z. Steinway, the last family member to be president of Steinway & Sons, a student of history and a member of the Greater Astoria Historical Society. The stories of the Steinway family and business are from a series of conversations and generous access to his family's collections at Steinway Hall.

Finally, a special thank-you to Debbie Van Cura, who not only has assisted in so many ways with this project, but whose family also lived in Long Island City for three generations and whose pool of knowledge and insight is so valuable in assessing the community and what makes it special.

INTRODUCTION

*A*sk one hundred people from the neighborhood who their favorite character is, and you will get one hundred different answers. But there is one common denominator: everyone is quick to share the story about these characters.

These stories, often passed down from generation to generation, are told as a matter of history, making the character's legends. Naturally, we want to believe they are true. So they become an essential part of our oral and written folklore. They become part of a community's culture—the legends or stories that make us unique.

Historic Tales of Long Island City is composed of exciting people, places and things. These stories are all part of the history of Long Island City. They give us a sense of where this community started and how it developed through the years, as well as a look into its future. These stories ground us in an identity of people who used their talents to make this neighborhood a good place to live. Their imaginations left us a legacy as "LIC: A World of Creativity."

The people and places in this collection all come from the communities of Steinway, Astoria Village, Ravenswood, Dutch Kills, Hunters Point, Sunnyside and Blissville. These neighborhoods were once part of the independent city of Long Island City (1870–98).

Read through the stories of people who searched for Eden on earth. Enjoy reading about Captain Kidd, and discover who Vernon Boulevard is named for and how vital the Steinway family was to our community. Do you know the story of why some vestibules have grape leaves on their tiles? Read the story about Gustave Mathews. If you are looking for a nostalgic story about Christmas, you will find it in these pages. Finally, you can quell your curiosity about some of the mayors of the independent city of Long Island City. You won't be disappointed by a particular legend of the Blissville Banshee.

The book is organized chronologically from 1640 through the twenty-first century. It is broken down into sections covering "Hallets Cove," the "Village of Astoria: Long Island City," "Gotham's Suburb" and ending with "LIC: The Cradle of Creativity." Among these stories, you will find some places you have visited, people you know or ideas that you always wondered about in each area. Please be aware that some spellings of names and places are different throughout the book—for example, Hallett and Hallet and Hellgate and Hell Gate. Wherever possible, we have retained the spelling found in the original documents of the period.

Originally a newspaper column titled "Legends of Long Island City," this fascinating and little-known past of New York's third city is compiled and published together here for the first time. Although the general order is chronological, each story can be read independently or, as they were written, randomly. Guaranteed, it's a slice of Gotham you have never seen before.

So get comfortable in your favorite chair and enjoy the *Historic Tales of Long Island City*!

—Greater Astoria Historical Society

PART I

Hallets Cove
(1640–1840)

Chapter 1

IN THE BEGINNING

*A*lthough it was named for a Bronx community, under the feet of Long Island City is one of the most ancient rock formations on the planet: Fordham gneiss. The rock is similar to the Canadian Shield, the geologists' label for the lands around Hudson Bay. It forms the core of the North American continent. It is more than 1.1 billion years old. Even earlier, 4.6 billion years ago, it was initially sand and silt from volcanic ash that filled an ancient sea that became sandstone during the Precambrian era, a time so distant life had hardly started.

Approximately 230 million years ago (even before the Atlantic Ocean existed), Africa was jammed against New England in a collision so powerful that it built a mountain chain that towered forty thousand feet. The Everest range, the highest mountain today, was about half as tall. The sandstone trapped under the roots of that mountain, under enormous pressure, metamorphosed into much harder rock, gneiss. It was repeatedly folded into swirls of contorted bands of black and gray layers, which we can see today. This testifies to the immense geologic forces that formed them under incredible heat and pressure.

Over time, the range weathered away, and Africa drifted east. Finally, about 160 million years ago, only stumps and those ancient peaks' cores remained. The glaciers, the next major geologic force in our region, spent several million years marching back and forth over the landscape. Each pass scraped up what was left of the mountains until, for the most part, they were far below sea level. In Long Island City, the bedrock that remains at

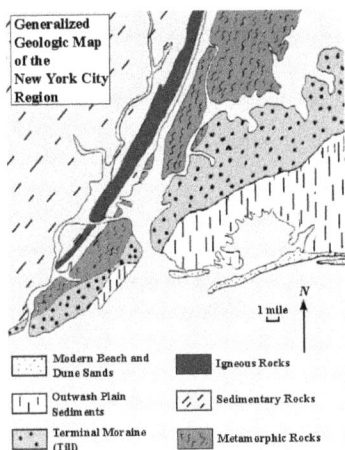

Geologic map of New York City region. *David Leveson, Brooklyn College, CUNY.*

the surface is found at a few spots along a narrow band between 21st Street and the East River. Scattered outcroppings are in Astoria Park, Ravenswood and Hunters Point, at 12th Street and 43rd Road.

Researchers believe that the ice sheet was taller than the Empire State Building. It both lowered the sea level and trapped a good portion of our planet's fresh water. After its last retreat, the ocean rose and drowned nearby streams known today as East River, Dutch Kills and Newtown Creek. As they were isolated and refreshed daily by the unpolluted tides, fish and shellfish bred in those shallow, fertile waters. Beavers built dams in this watery wilderness (the slight incline on Northern Boulevard and Woodside Avenue was reported to be one such mound). Newtown Creek had abundant clams the size of dinner plates.

During the excavation of Anable Basin at 45th Road and Vernon Avenue, a large mastodon bone (found at a depth of thirteen feet and four hundred yards from the river) created something of a sensation when excavated in 1868. It was later exhibited for years in the window of a local store. Unfortunately, the creature probably died when it became trapped in the mud along the riverbank, perhaps between ten thousand and fifteen thousand years ago.

The rest of Long Island City east of 21st Street formed from glacial deposits of gravel and sand. The latest glacier was just sixteen thousand years ago—just the blink of an eye in Earth history.

The earliest descriptions tell of a landscape of swamps and ponds. Geese, ducks and other fowl nested in the grassy hammocks. Rocky outcrops broke the expanse of meadow and provided a base for stands of trees and bush. A "waving abundance" of salt hay, which would later be prized by the European herdsmen for its rich nutritional value to sheep and cattle, grew along the river. As recently as 160 years ago, Hunters Point was a small island (about three square blocks and bisected by today's Vernon Boulevard) surrounded by a vast low-lying meadow flooded at every tide by the East River.

The solitude was broken by the Dutch when their first deeds were granted in 1643.

Chapter 2

FINDING EDEN

From the wilderness unto the great sea
toward the going down of the sun, shall be yours.
—Joshua 1:4

S imilar to other immigrant settlements dotting the coast up to New England, our community's earliest recorded history starts with a small group of English settlers led by preacher Francis Doughty, who received a land grant to settle a town at the headwaters of Newtown Creek.

As other earliest settlers in Flushing, Jamaica and Hallets Cove discovered, they chose a location adjacent to a Native American village, in this case Maspeth. This area was already linked to other areas by a network of paths, had clearings for farming and had streams rich in both fish and game. Foreshadowing our modern society, their community was a mixture of peoples: both English and Dutch, as well as Native and African.

They selected the head of Newtown Creek for two additional reasons: its convenience as a waterborne highway leading to the seacoast and its seclusion from the prying eyes of authority.

Although Doughty and his congregation's stated goal was to seek Eden in the New World, this was during an age when religious upheaval challenged both moral orthodoxy and civic authority. The Dutch were aware of the risks in welcoming the English into the colony, and as feared, they proved troublesome, quarreling with one another and with the authorities over laws, land and religion. When their neighbors tried to reclaim disputed

Colonists from Europe with a pastor conducting a prayer service in the mid-seventeenth century. *Public domain.*

land, they pushed back with stronger methods only hinted at in the historical record.

Swept off their land by Indigenous uprisings that spread throughout New Amsterdam, the English settlers doggedly returned. Finally, after angering the authorities over both smuggling (and hiding import duties from the government) and claiming lands the Dutch did not believe were theirs, the exasperated government terminated their land grant. Undeterred, they fought back with lawsuits before playing their last card, declaring allegiance to New England and helping to bring down the Dutch government.

After the government changed, they continued to plague the authorities. When virulent religious revivals swept New England and Long Island Sound, their settlement was home to the most radical. A Quaker sect called Case's Crew filled local jails with ecstatic cult members charged with, among other things, seducing housewives from husbands and children.

Yet within their settlement were others, such as Thomas Wandell and Humphrey Clay, among the most successful and notorious merchants in New York who did business with smugglers and pirates. Wandell's tobacco plantation, now the expansive gentle acres of Calvary Cemetery, gives us a hint of wealth accumulated by uncertain means. Clay, whose family résumé included expulsion from Connecticut and testimony in London Chancery leading to the conviction and hanging of pirate Captain Kidd, owned an extensive group of slaves, perhaps hinting at a significant factoring business involving smuggled goods on the creek. Constant traffic between their two operations led to the first bridge over Newtown Creek, which was called, for its toll, Penny Bridge.

As a forecast of modern New York, their community attracted a diverse group of people from around the world. But when the edgy, chaotic frontier spirit of New York began to wind down, around the turn of the eighteenth century, the colony at Maspeth Landing suddenly dissolved in search of new opportunities along the ever-shifting frontier. Some settled in upstate New York and others moved to New Jersey's Hopewell Valley, while a few disappeared into history.

They left behind an abandoned Quaker meetinghouse, a Native American village, a handful of dwellings and, perhaps, a lingering spirit in the air—that of a burning vision of Manifest Destiny, a dream whose roots they found in their fervid interpretation of scriptures.

Enter DeWitt Clinton, who inherited one of those dwellings, a mansion at the head of Newtown Creek, from his father-in-law, Walter Franklin, a Quaker related to the Bowne family in Flushing. Clinton was undoubtedly familiar with the dreams of his now semi-mythical predecessors. But, unlike them, he had the resources to finally access the "American Eden"—that vast, pristine promise of the American continent.

A scion of one of the leading families in New York State, Clinton's résumé of accomplishment and list of entry to those powerful and connected was second to none. Yet he focused his attention on what was to be his life's work: access to the Inland Empire. Led by the dreams of those who once lived in our community, he was about to write another chapter in our legacy. It was Clinton who was to make New York City the "Empire City."

Chapter 3

350 YEARS OF CUTTING EDGE

*T*he ancient millstones of Queens Plaza, which some people claim as the oldest European artifacts in the borough, became hot items in local news. Are they 350 years old, as the record claims? Did they come from Holland? Perhaps both points are open to debate, but one thing is sure: their past—as well as their future—is indeed a mystery.

New York governor Edmund Andros encouraged Parliament to pass the Bolting Act of 1678, granting New York merchants a monopoly for milling grain and building ships to export flour and cornmeal to England. Historians credit this legislative act as the foundation for the city's fortune. As a tribute to the importance of milling in the city's history, New York's coat of arms has two flour barrels.

Several tidal mills dotted the shoreline of Queens—the mouth of virtually every local stream had one—but the oldest mill, built between 1643 and 1654, was in our community. Called Jorissen's Mill after its owner, Burger Jorissen, it is within the railroad yards north of Queens Plaza and east of Northern Boulevard. The end of 41st Avenue in Dutch Kills marked the approximate location of the milldam.

As the incoming tide flowed up Dutch Kills into a pond behind the mill, its force turned millstones that ground grain or corn. About five hours later, when the tide started to flow out, the water from the millpond was released. The millstones again ground grain, but this time with the wheels going in the opposite direction. It was very efficient using the same water twice.

Millstone from Burger Jorissen Tide Mill (mid-1660s) embedded in Queens Plaza, circa 1990. *Greater Astoria Historical Society.*

Burger Jorissen's mill lasted for a century and a half after his death. Starting at 48th Street and running to Queens Plaza, the ditch draining water from a marsh into the millpond was visible along Northern Boulevard as late as 1900. But the tide mill was little used after 1820, as local farmers grew fruit in orchards and vegetables or flowers in greenhouses. In addition, cultivation and milling of wheat or corn gravitated to the Midwest.

The Long Island Rail Road found the former millpond the perfect right of way for a rail line to Hunters Point. It filled in the grassy marsh and tore down the remains of the gristmill in 1861. The following year, the Hunters Point and Flushing Turnpike (later Northern Boulevard) was opened along the millpond's edge. The gentle curve of Northern Boulevard between Queens Plaza and Woodside Avenue traces the millpond's former course.

The Payntar family, who owned land on what would later be Queens Plaza, placed the two millstones between their home and the turnpike (Northern Boulevard).

With Long Island City's creation in 1870, the area's gradual transformation from rural farms to a modern street grid was assured. Work started in 1901 on the Queensboro Bridge and Queens Plaza, where a network of elevated train lines and highways linked Brooklyn, Astoria and Flushing. Then, in 1903, the Pennsylvania Railroad started building the Sunnyside Rail Yards, connecting the area with New England and New Jersey.

This commercial development soon forced the Payntar family out of their ancestral home, originally built in about 1720 on Jorissen's 1640 home foundations. When Northern Boulevard's roadway was raised twenty feet in 1901, the house disappeared behind an embankment, giving kids from nearby Long Island City High School an excellent cover to break in and set fires. The family had no choice but to tear down the ancient landmark in January 1913. In its place went up a commercial loft building (which was, in turn, torn down in about 2000 for the tunnel project linking the Long Island Rail Road to Grand Central Station).

It is undoubtedly a minor miracle that the two millstones did not disappear. Still, likely one of the Payntars prevailed on the Bank of Manhattan to embed them in a traffic island near Queens Plaza North sometime around 1920.

The redevelopment of Queens Plaza brought the millstones back in the news. The community expressed concern for both their safety and condition. A photo from a brochure published by Long Island Savings Bank dated about 1940, when they were about 150 years old, shows the millstones looking almost like new. However, exposed to the elements, traffic and pollution, they have deteriorated dramatically in the past decade.

When Queens Plaza was reimagined, the community expressed concern for the millstones' safety. Ultimately, they were mounted on pedestals after holes were drilled into them. Subsequently, they were graffitied, and unsupported edges were broken off, cemented back in place and ultimately disappeared.

Several suggestions are being discussed to find a safe home for them, but everyone agrees on one point: they must stay within the community. The beauty of Queens Plaza is that you have the millstones, railroad, loft buildings and recent development—350 years of cutting-edge enterprise—in just one spot. Where else in New York City do you have that?

Chapter 4

CATHERINE OF QUEENS

*U*ncovering or celebrating the past is usually fun, but when stubborn myths triumph over truth, it can take an ugly turn. Take Queen Catherine of Braganza and her alleged association with the Borough of Queens.

When the British Crown asserted control in New York with the 1683 Charter of Liberties and Privileges, the only name in the document was his "Royall Highnesse James Duke of Yorke Albany & Lord Proprietor," who was given authority over the colony by his brother Charles II. The charter established counties whose names echoed locations in England (Westchester, Suffolk and York) and the titles of royal offices (king, queen and duchess). The motto on the official seal of New York refers to New York as *Eboraci*, the Latin name given by the Romans who established the city of York, England. It was a term not used in association with the Duke of York.

For two hundred years, no reference was made to linking those county names to specific individuals. The myth started innocently enough, similar to little George Washington and the apple tree or Betsy Ross sewing the first American flag. In the same spirit, names mentioned in the charter began to be associated with other officeholders (Kings County for King James; Dutchess County for Mary of Modena, Duchess of York; and Queens County for King James's wife, Catherine of Braganza, who was from Portugal).

What started as harmless fun grew into something far different. In the 1990s, a group called the Friends of Queen Catherine seized on

A modern (1999) stained-glass picture of Queen Catherine at the 46th Street train platform. *Stephan Grütering, 2019.*

this folktale and, perhaps in an attempt to publicize Expo '98, a world's fair in Lisbon, Portugal, suggested building a five-story statue of Queen Catherine, mounted on a fifteen-foot base on the East River, across from the United Nations. At just under one hundred feet, it was to be the second-tallest statue in New York, eclipsed only by the three-hundred-foot Statue of Liberty.

Mainstream historians were split. Some supported the statue, while others challenged its backers to provide evidence of Catherine's involvement with the Borough of Queens. Her supporters spun tales comparing Queen Catherine favorably to Lady Liberty, a symbol of freedom.

However, their effort faltered when her family's extensive connection to the transatlantic slave trade was made public. Nearly half of all African slaves in the Middle Passage were destined for Portuguese Brazil, creating the highest concentration of slaves since the Roman Empire.

After her husband's death, Catherine got entangled in British politics and, frustrated, returned to her home country. With these facts, it seems unlikely the British ever considered her a candidate to be officially honored as the namesake of any portion of a colony.

Although the statue project stopped amid lawsuits and recrimination (a small-scale model facing America was built for Expo '98), Catherine's association with Queens has stubbornly remained. More than twenty years after the controversy, a 2019 tourism brochure stated that Queens "is actually named for Queen Catherine of Braganza," a "fact" also repeated on Wikipedia and, increasingly, elsewhere.

Moreover, in 1999, Queen Catherine was permanently immortalized in a stained-glass image at the 46th Street platform of the 7 train and is viewed by thousands daily.

Chapter 5

PARSING MAN FROM LEGEND

F or three hundred years, the debate has raged about Captain William Kidd. Was he or was he not a pirate? Was he an innocent man, a scapegoat for a way of life that had outlived its usefulness and no longer was of benefit to those in power? The privateer and his cargo of uncertain background (whether a duty was paid or not) were no longer welcome at the king's ports. Kidd's execution drew to a close the era of the freebooting merchant warrior.

The details of Kidd's life are, for the most part, missing. People in his profession wisely did not leave diaries. Nevertheless, some hints and fragments form a picture. History may have stamped him, rightly or not, a pirate, but he clearly did not fit our image of a bloodthirsty buccaneer. No earring, parrot or bandana for him! Kidd was the cream of society, noted for both his fashionable style (his parlor boasted the largest Persian carpet in town) as well as his public works (he lent his ship's block and tackle to lift stones for the Trinity Church steeple).

There is no doubt that he spent time on Long Island. From Brooklyn to the Hamptons, families handed down personal legends. The Meseroles of Bushwick even claim that Kidd was betrothed to one of their clan. So when he returned from the Caribbean and received news that his fiancée had died, Kidd was grief-stricken. They say his sloop was spotted often tied up to a dock in Bushwick Creek near her gravesite.

Newtown Creek had a particularly nasty reputation as a harbor for all sorts of mysterious types, who, as one account would have us believe, lived

A fanciful early twentieth-century depiction of Captain Kidd. *Jean-Leon Gerome Ferris, 1911.*

in caves hollowed out of the clay under the bluffs of what was later called Pottery Beach. For years, the skeleton of a ship lay broken on the creek banks, lured, as rumor had it, to its fate by the locals. What happened to its crew and cargo were matters of wild speculation.

Two people within Kidd's circle on Newtown Creek during those unsettled times in the late 1600s were Thomas Wandell and Humphrey Clay. Both shared close family ties with each other, having married sisters.

Wandell was a member of the mercantile elite that controlled New York during that period. He owned a house near Kidd's in Hanover Square and a large parcel of land on Staten Island (Governor Carteret of New Jersey was a partner). Of interest to us was his Long Island country estate (a plantation that later became Calvary Cemetery). Wandell was a prominent leader in Newtown, serving on juries and holding public office.

Clay, in Bushwick just across the creek from Wandell, had a decidedly more checkered past. He and his wife were tossed out of Connecticut for selling guns and rum to Native Americans. Their inn had a reputation for attracting the region's worst riffraff. Perhaps through the suggestion of his brothers (who were ship captains), Clay soon relocated to Newtown Creek's more welcoming shores. We don't quite have a clear picture of how he earned his livelihood, but there seems to have been a lot of activity between Clay and Wandell, for they started a ferry service that ran between their wharves. The ferry was later replaced by Penny Bridge (so named for its one-cent toll). The census of the time showed that Clay owned a large number of slaves.

In the closing years of the 1600s, Clay's son, also named Humphrey, was listed as a crew member who sailed with Kidd on his last ill-fated Indian Ocean expedition. The High Court of Admiralty recorded Clay's interrogation in London, resulting in Kidd and his crew being arrested. Granted clemency for his testimony, Clay painted Kidd as a hunted man who, in a desperate bid to buy his way out of trouble, left caches of money and treasure along the coast of New England and Long Island Sound. Partly on this testimony, Kidd was convicted of piracy and was executed.

Chapter 6

PLAGUE CITY

e likely arrived on a sloop, a swift, trim vessel that was the mainstay for trade along the Atlantic coast from the Caribbean to New England. It was 1668, and New York, recently forced into the British Empire, was the newly minted clearinghouse for a network of international traffic that ranged from the Red Sea to Port Royal, Jamaica. Goods were hurriedly lifted from the hold and carted off and then quickly replaced with cargo flagged for new destinations. Money was counted, with a nod and wink; paperwork was signed; and they were again on their way.

However, one seaman was left behind, feverish, and soon after falling into a swoon, he died—a nameless soul for the city's Potters Field. A mosquito discovered the man while awaiting burial. Later hitching a ride across the East River on a farmer's pirogue, it laid eggs in one of the many marshes along Newtown Creek.

With Long Island City's network of creeks and standing ponds, danger from fever was especially keen. About this time, John Scudder dammed English Kills on Newtown Creek with a tide mill. The stagnant millpond harbored mosquitoes that sickened local residents. A neighbor, John Hart, died "of fever and ague." A near-riot by his neighbors forced Scudder to drain the pond.

Fearful of more problems, the owner of an adjacent mill on Dutch Kills, another tributary on Newtown Creek, dug out a ditch (called Berger's Sluice) channeling the streams that fed his tide mill. The course of that effort is now

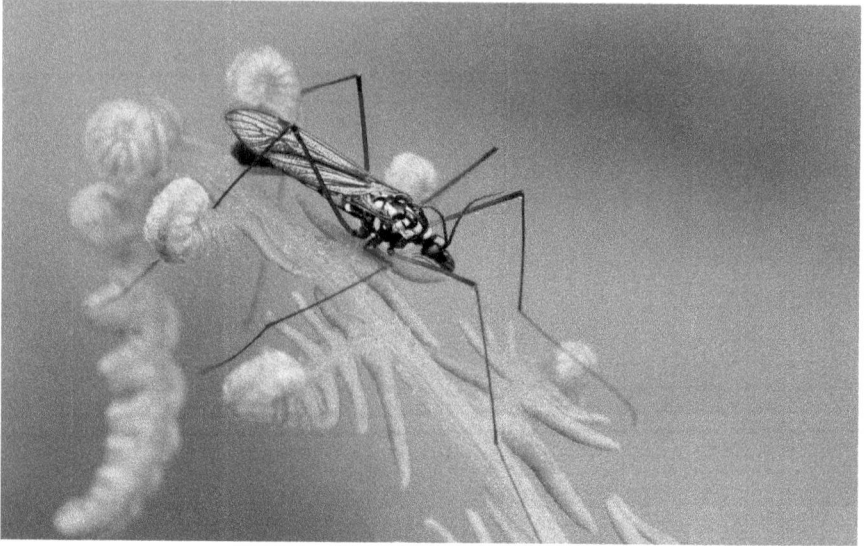

Mosquitoes are often carrier of sickness. *Pixio Creative Commons.*

traced by the gentle curve of Northern Boulevard between Woodside and Queens Plaza. New York had experienced its first epidemic. It was destined to become a harbor for tropical diseases for the next 250 years.

The region held its breath each spring, anticipating a sudden panic if residents had to flee from yet another horrific plague. In 1828, during one of the plagues, Greenwich Village was built up. Washington Square was the dumping ground for tens of thousands of plague victims (and later the other parks dotting Manhattan's Midtown). The autobiography of Grant Thorburn describes his work in Manhattan tending to the sick and the recovery of bodies during the recurring epidemics that periodically emptied the city. He later moved to Astoria to run one of the nation's largest flower nurseries at that time.

In 1847, when New York City purchased land for a quarantine hospital near today's Rainey Park, concerns that patients would contaminate Sunswick Creek rose to a fevered pitch. Locals from Astoria Village rioted and then torched it before opening day. A hearing was called. No one was arrested.

As the area developed in the 1860s, Sunswick Creek became a severe health hazard. Annual outbreaks of illness became endemic within the communities of Dutch Kills and Ravenswood. Often, more than half of the students from the community missed school, being ill at home. Local employers suggested that workers show up for alternate days to build up immunity. One year in the 1870s, most of the police force called in sick.

This crisis was one of the factors prompting the creation of Long Island City. Residents now had the muscle to finance draining the entire swamp. The effort stretched over fifty years and was only completed about 1920 when muck from the Manhattan subway construction built up Queens Plaza to eliminate the last pockets of contagion.

Postscript: A grandson of Hart and a granddaughter of Scudder later married. After the passage of ten generations and 350 years, they share many thousands of descendants—including the author of this account!

Chapter 7

SHOW ME THE MONEY

*Y*ou can go to Dutch Kills Green and see two millstones. One was a runner, which turned, and the other was a bedstone, which was fixed. The faces of the stones, scored with furrows and ridges, marked with such colorful names as skirt, breast, harp, fly and Spanish cross, have remained silent for five generations. They are the tangible relic of something that goes back a dozen generations. They are remnants of a tide mill and are among the earliest European artifacts in Queens County.

In 1674, New York governor Edmund Andros convened landowners and businessmen in New York's first actual legislature. They were tasked with reviving a failed city rife with contagion, crime and corruption. Businesses were dormant; beaver had been hunted to all but extinction, and devalued agricultural product was routinely adulterated with chaff and inferior grains. Nevertheless, it was Andros who set in stone New York's partnership of business and government. In every real sense, he is the true "Father of New York." The result of their labor was so crucial that it's displayed on the New York City Coat of Arms to this day: flour barrels.

A series of laws, called Bolting Acts, covered New York's largest export, wheat flour and cornmeal, and set strict milling quality standards and transportation standards. Export quality was checked. Furthermore, all outgoing and incoming ships had to stop in New York for cargo inspection. As a result, Long Island farmers, East River tide mills, warehousemen, shipbuilders, coopers and merchants were suddenly inundated with more business than they could handle. Within a generation, the city's economy

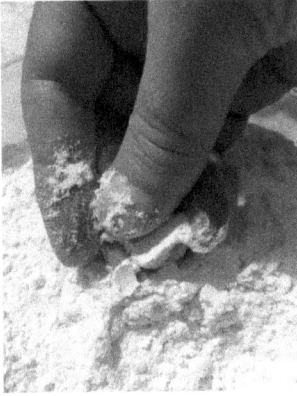

Testing the quality of flour.
Author's collection.

and housing grew threefold, shipbuilding fivefold and cattle tenfold. New York launched on a trajectory of growth enjoyed to this day.

The landscape of Long Island was transformed. Sleepy hamlets along Newtown Creek witnessed a steady stream of incoming barges full of corn and wheat and outgoing casks of flour and meal. Tide mills on English Kills and Dutch Kills ran 24/7 with an inexhaustible energy source from the tides that dutifully raised and lowered millponds each day.

Former malarial marshland was drained and dug out to increase the size and power of the tide millponds. The gentle curve of Northern Boulevard between Queens Plaza and Woodside traces Burger's Sluice, a ditch dug to supply water power to the Queens Plaza tide mill. Tide mills spread across Long Island and Brooklyn (most notably in Red Hook). In Queens, they were built at Halletts Cove, near LaGuardia Airport, farther out to Flushing, Alley Pond and perhaps within the Flushing Meadow valley.

The primordial forest in Queens was cut down as farmers began to expand crop acreage destined for a global market. New York was now firmly plugged into the international trading network. The semitropical climate of Queens made for a long growing season. Soils of rich loam gave it the title the "Granary of America." Neighboring Flushing was dubbed the "Birthplace of American Horticulture," and in Newtown (Elmhurst), the legendary Newtown Pippin apple, which could withstand the Atlantic crossing in casks, became America's first high-value fruit export.

So what about those millstones in Dutch Kills Green? Everyone who is a businessperson, or a New Yorker, should make a pilgrimage to see them, for here, the New York that we know started. The millers were known as a sturdy and shrewd group; it was they who bequeathed us our legendary "New York attitude." And the source of the gesture "show me the money" by rubbing the thumb and forefingers together? That was how the miller tested a batch of flour for quality.

Chapter 8

HARD MEN

In the early years of our republic, New York already stood out as a place cut from a different cloth. Virginia might lay claim as Europe's first outpost, Boston was the cradle of revolution and Philadelphia's population outranked all others. Still, everyone's eyes instinctively turned to New York—for it was here that the new nation's spirit was conceived. But if it were not for events that transpired in western Queens, our republic could have died before leaving its cradle.

After the Revolution, New York was in ruins, for it was devastated by fire and depopulated by occupation. But it did recover quickly as its outlying districts, such as Long Island City, the engine of renewal, remained intact. Throughout war and subsequent peace, our tide mills never stopped. Instead, they were ready to provide the spark to restart the region's economy.

Throughout that occupation, the British kept those mills working overtime. Enormous quantities of bread were needed to feed a hungry army, and farmers were forced to hand over a portion of their harvest. It was no secret that the mills played a vital role in supporting the British war effort. Yankee whaleboat men from as far away as Connecticut made periodic raids to Queens to destroy those mills (and rob their owners, who were making a fortune while their neighbors were impoverished).

When garrisons were set up to protect them, the millers, with a long reputation as hard, tough men, took this as an opportunity to make yet more money, for they built taverns adjoining the mills. Quickly becoming social centers of sorts, these places soon spawned wartime fraternization between

A statue of a man on a horse. *Author's collection.*

troops and young ladies of local farmers—something that created deep bitterness among the colonials. John Ryerson, who ran the tide mill at Dutch Kills, unwisely stayed on after the conflict and was murdered in his taproom during an argument. In 1902, during excavations for Long Island City High School, his coffin was unearthed at 29th Street and 41st Avenue.

Our community also played an influential role in ending the conflict between Great Britain and the United States. A copy of the original treaty was carried across the Atlantic and presented to the American government (then in New York) by Major John Delafield, a merchant. He lived in a magnificent mansion in Ravenswood. The war was over, but for many, there would be no peace. The old order was gone. Some families, such as the Blackwells, were split by the conflict. Others, such as the pro-British Halletts, were forced to sell their property and almost swept away in the tides of that time. With some irony, the Hallett Farm was purchased by a semi-retired Continental brigadier general, Ebenezer Stevens, a participant in the Boston Tea Party and witness to the Battles of Saratoga and Yorktown, both pivotal events in the road to independence.

General Stevens organized the defense of New York during the War of 1812, a conflict called by some the "Second War of Independence." He supervised the building of a series of forts (in Astoria and on the offshore Hell Gate islands), which stopped the British from sailing through Long Island Sound, landing an army and marching on to New York to destroy it—as they had done with the burning of our capital, Washington.

New York's end could have well ended the republic, too. Coupled with New England's active desire to have peace with Britain, the loss of Washington and New York would have made the nation's future uncertain. Thus, our community can lay claim to halting a precipitous chain of events that could have led to the dissolution of the United States.

Jefferson's 1803 Louisiana Purchase and the end of the War of 1812 opened up the vast interior of the American continent. At the head of Newtown Creek, within the sound of the humming clatter of the tide mill at English Kills, a man sat thinking while looking at a map. His name was DeWitt Clinton.

He was to bring the Inland Empire to the Empire City.

Chapter 9

LIEUTENANT BARRY, PART I

THE HONORS OF WAR

O n a small hill in Hellgate, behind the Hallett barn and overlooking the cove, Reverend Josiah Bloomer, St. James Church pastor, opened his Book of Common Prayer. A Liturgy of the Dead was about to begin. The event was noteworthy enough to be mentioned in the *New-York Gazette*.

The deceased was Lieutenant William Barry, likely a younger son from minor Irish Protestant gentry. In the tradition of "Wild Geese," as young Irish soldiers were called, he exchanged slim opportunities at home to become a soldier of fortune. Before the Revolution, he fought for the Prussian army until he resigned in 1778 to try his luck in the American War for Independence.

Upon arriving in Britain's rebellious colonies, he served briefly as a lieutenant in the King's Orange Rangers and then as a captain in Ireland's Volunteers. Here, Barry saw the grit of war. He was present during the expedition to Portsmouth, Virginia (1779), when British general Cornwallis looted the colony of supplies destined for Washington's army, and the Siege of Charleston (1780), in which the gates to the South were opened to the British in the worst American defeat of the war.

Barry seemed to chart his own narrative, whimsically disappearing during the Portsmouth operation only to reappear without horse and equipment. His antics must have continued, for during the Charleston siege, papers were filed seeking a court-martial. Barry issued countercharges claiming lack of pay (nearly $80,000 in today's currency). Finally, he was found guilty of some charges. Facing reprimand, he quit the service.

A year later, in 1781, with the war in its sixth year, the British knew that stalemate was a road to defeat. Warfare voraciously consumed cash. Former enemies eyed opportunities to pluck pieces of the empire. Moreover, the locals, rebel and Loyalist alike, were chafing under the heel of an occupying army that left a growing trail of angry farmers with crops confiscated, merchants with goods pilfered and fathers with daughters of uncertain virtue.

A portrait of a British soldier during the American Revolution. *Shutterstock.*

The British High Command drafted an impressive array of seventy local units, but it was only a paper army. As a newly minted lieutenant with the Loyal Foresters, Barry was not taken back out of leniency but desperation. With only fifty men, his unit prompted their commanding officer, Lieutenant Colonel Connolly, to travel to Virginia in an attempt to muster more recruits. Their colonel's absence must have provided the perfect environment for Barry. Idle soldiers, with plenty of cash and time, are a recipe for mischief. There is little doubt Barry was the most popular fellow in camp.

It must have been a shock that Barry caught a chill in the early days of autumn and died suddenly—perhaps when news arrived that commanding officer Connolly and the British army in Virginia were prisoners of Washington and the French at Yorktown. Within months, they knew that Washington would be back in New York, ready for the final battle. Then, although the treaty would not be signed for two years, the war was over.

A small knot of men stood in a circle at the Hellgate, wigs powdered, heads bowed, resplendent in scarlet tunics and gold braid. But it was their eyes that would catch our attention—the eyes of veterans who can never find words to speak of the bond of brotherhood and the random horrors and madness of war itself. They were burying not only their friend "with the honors of war" but also the dreams of Britain's rule over the Thirteen Colonies.

They also left behind in Halletts Cove a mysterious white marble stone. It is the topic of our next chapter.

Chapter 10

LIEUTENANT BARRY, PART II

A SLAB IN THE WALL

A special thank-you to Susan Rahyab for her research assistance.

T he Greater Astoria Historical Society got a call a few years ago from a homeowner who lived on a hill and had recently removed a portion of his yard to create street-level parking. Lying flat, several feet under the surface (the exact depth after the lapse of time is vague), he found a white marble slab. He disposed of the excavated soil but cemented the stone into the retaining wall as an ornamental novelty.

After taking measurements and photographs, we immediately suspected it was likely a gravestone (an observation later affirmed probable by tombstone experts). It was found near where a soldier—Lieutenant Barry of the Loyal Foresters—was buried two and a half centuries ago. Could his wealthy, heartbroken friends, who buried him (as newspapers of the time stated) with the "honors of war," have commissioned a white marble gravestone in his honor?

Gravestone historian Elise Madeleine Ciregna, who has examined the stone via photographs, stated, "I have consulted with several other experts and colleagues of mine about this intriguing stone. I do believe—and my colleagues agree—that this may be a late-18th century gravestone…[as opposed to a decorative ornamental or garden piece] because it appears to be in a 'slab' shape, which is really only used for headstone purposes in the 18th and 19th centuries."

But she cautions, "The stone, [at 10 inches] is extremely thick…much thicker by far than any marble gravestone I have ever seen—and much thicker than it would have needed to be. Typically, early marbles in a slab form are usually no more than 2 inches thick. [Also] there were few marble workers in early America capable of producing this nicely carved stone [and there is] no signature or legible design/lettering."

She also further decried a proper archaeological excavation to determine evidence of human remains.

Every argument can be met with a counterargument. Perhaps a stone slab intended to be cut into several slabs for multiple burials was "requisitioned" by a squad of troops. Maybe with no money or time for an engraver, a tribute was painted on the stone. (Letter "shapes" are found, but it is unclear if they are simply staining from the soil that creates optional illusions of letters.) Is its location, discovered a few feet underground, merely the result of hurriedly tossing a stone into landfill or an attempt to disguise the grave and protect it from desecration by hiding it?

All burial stone arguments sound reasonable if we remember that the interment was conducted in the closing chapter of the Revolution when the British occupation began to unravel. However, extraordinary claims require extraordinary evidence.

The soil removal makes it all but impossible to confirm a burial since remains such as buttons and bone fragments were lost. All that we have is a stone—and it is blank. Barring a battery of tests to confirm possible lettering pigment or taking a sample of the stone to determine its origin, this riddle will likely remain unsolved. Money is not granted for these things.

The marble slab found in a yard excavation, circa 1990. *Greater Astoria Historical Society.*

Chapter 11

TO ALL A GOOD NIGHT!

*T*he coachman arrived in Chelsea promptly at 7:00 a.m. The wife supervised loading food and gifts in the wagon's boot and, with the help of a footman, climbed aboard with her young child, bundled from the biting cold. Her husband took his place on the facing seat. The coachman cracked his whip. The horses, heads held high, livery polished and gleaming in the early morning light, started their journey.

> *He sprang to his sleigh, to his team gave a whistle, and away they all flew like the down of a thistle. Now dash away! dash away! dash away all!*

It would take hours to cover the route on rutted roads; to wait for the Hell Gate Ferry in numbing, biting cold; and to journey the final muddy leg to their destination in Queens, at a location described today as on Hazen Street where Woodside and Astoria meet.

The mother held her drowsing son close. He was born in difficult times during the War for Independence. But now peace was declared, and a new nation and a new people were taking the stage to define a fresh identity. The old tradition of throwing one's home open to the rowdy crowds on Christmas was being replaced by something new: the holiday was now an opportunity for families to get together and share meals, gifts and time together. This year, they were going to visit her husband's cousins in Queens.

To numbed travelers, the house, though old, was warm, inviting and full of family. The yule log crackled in the fire. Garlands of holly, ivy, mistletoe and rosemary provided a pleasant holiday scent.

"Merry Old Santa Claus,"
from the January 1, 1881
edition of *Harper's Weekly*.
Thomas, public domain.

*The stockings were hung by the chimney with care in hopes that St. Nicholas
soon would be there.*

Dinner was served at noon. The aroma of food, which had been sitting
on the table to cool for an hour, was mouth-watering. Plates were passed
family style. Dessert included cakes, cookies, jellies and plum pudding, all
downed with punch. After the meal, they sang carols including "The First
Noel," "God Rest Ye Merry Gentlemen" and "Joy to the World." Games
such as blind man's bluff followed. Meanwhile, the coachman, lost in his
own thoughts by the fire, smoked his pipe.

*His eyes—how they twinkled! His dimples, how merry! His cheeks were like
roses, his nose like a cherry! His droll little mouth was drawn up like a bow,
and the beard on his chin was as white as the snow. The stump of a pipe
he held tight in his teeth, and the smoke, it encircled his head like a wreath.*

40

After fun and frolic, everyone sat down to a substantial supper—and a mighty bowl of wassail. Winter days being short, the sun was already kissing the horizon. The little boy, exhausted by the festivities, soon fell asleep on his mother's breast during the long ride home.

> *The children were nestled all snug in their beds While visions of sugar-plums danced in their heads; the moon on the breast of the new-fallen snow gave a luster of midday to objects below.*

The little boy never forgot that evening. Years later, as a parent, he wanted to share its magic with his own children. So Clement Clarke Moore wrote "A Visit from St. Nicholas," making a Queens Christmas the template for a nation.

Chapter 12

WHEN THE DITMARS FAMILY
LIVED ON DITMARS BOULEVARD

*W*hen they hear the name "Ditmars," most people associate the word with Astoria (which is correct), not Long Island City (which is incorrect). Astoria historically is a community of Greater Long Island City, and for this reason, the histories of both communities are intertwined. For example, the first mayor of Long Island City, Abram D. Ditmars, was born and grew up in Astoria, but he lived there while serving his term as mayor of his and our city, Long Island City.

The Ditmars family were among the first residents in Dutch Kills when Jan Jansen Ditmars (nicknamed "Flatnose") settled there in 1647. However, their tenure was brief, for they soon sold their property and moved to Flatbush, Brooklyn (where the name is spelled *Ditmas* to this day). Later, a branch moved back to Queens and settled in Jamaica, the birthplace of Abram's father, Dow (or Douwe) Ditmars, in 1771.

Dow, a Princeton graduate, briefly tried his hand at teaching. He then studied medicine and moved to British Guinea (modern Guyana) in South America. He returned to the States and bought a farm in 1816 at Hell Gate. The house, located at the corner of present-day Shore Road and Ditmars Boulevard, was built in the early 1700s. It was a prominent square brick structure on the waterfront with broad piazzas in the front and rear. There he practiced both farming and medicine. He died in 1860 at age ninety.

His son Abram was the first mayor of Long Island City. A respected attorney, he was instrumental in securing the Long Island City charter. During June 1870, residents across Long Island City participated in a series

Dow Ditmars's home (1719) on Shore Road, about 1900. *Greater Astoria Historical Society.*

of meetings that nominated candidates for various offices, including mayor. The Democrats nominated Ditmars of Astoria to head their ticket, and as they had a clear majority, he was virtually assured the office. As predicted, he won the election supported by a heavy turnout in Astoria and Bowery Bay (Astoria Heights).

Ditmars made a good impression at the outset by donating his two-year salary to the treasury. In the last months of 1870, the new mayor made a few appointments and set up committees. Although things began harmoniously enough, with all parties favoring Ditmars, trouble started when he proved too frugal and honest. Opposition quickly arose.

Politics in Long Island City soon became turbulent and disorderly. Everything from elections to taxes became mired in ongoing litigation and controversy. Corruption and graft quickly became the established order of the day. By 1873, Ditmars had been voted out of office by the "Ring" (as the local political machine was called).

When most of the proceeds from a $300,000 bond issue for a new water supply ended up in the pockets of political insiders who received a financial bonanza for water rights—without a single customer getting as much as a drop of water—the public's temperature reached the boiling point. Finally, the people had enough of fraud and waste.

In the election of 1875, Ditmars was successfully reelected mayor. Unfortunately, it was an empty victory. The Common Council of Long Island City, a creature of the Ring, soon made it clear that it would be hostile to any appointments or legislation he proposed. It was a stalemate. Disgusted, Ditmars abruptly resigned, leaving the Common Council president, John Quinn, as acting mayor. Ditmars promptly moved out of Long Island City to Brooklyn.

Chapter 13

THE HERALD OF
THE DAWN OF TODAY

*D*oes a community not follow a process of birth, growth and maturity into adulthood? Our four-hundred-year history neatly follows this pattern, with the center point being the decade around 1820. This marks the beginning of the modern era, or at least some sense of the modern era. The story of DeWitt Clinton and his wife, Maria Franklin, residents in a spacious mansion off Newtown Creek, illustrates the break from our community's past—and the beginning of our future.

Descended from the Underhill, Bowne, Seaman and Pearsall families, Maria undoubtedly heard stories of the colony and city of New York's struggles and rise to prominence. Although the rise of industry would soon change things, these families remained prominent in local social, political and business circles, as they had throughout the colonial period. Maria's parents rented their Manhattan townhouse to the American government as the nation's first Executive Mansion during the presidency of George Washington.

DeWitt Clinton was also born into an equally illustrious circle prominent in the political and social world of colonial New York. However, his family had quite a different focus than that of his wife, for it revolved around developing institutions and ideas that would soon be needed by the embryonic republic.

It is likely that no public official, past or present, has held as many offices as DeWitt Clinton, some concurrently: mayor of New York, lieutenant governor (and later governor) of New York State and United States senator. He ran for president in 1812, nearly beating James Madison. His interests carried over into the cultural (founder of the New-York Historical Society, reorganized the Academy of Fine Arts, elected a member of the American Antiquarian Society), educational (regent of the University of the State of New York) and scientific (New York fellow of the American Academy of Arts and Sciences) realms.

Although any one of the items listed would have earned him a firm Wiki entry, his crowning achievement was in linking New York to the continent's heartland by spearheading the development of the Erie Canal. As some called it, the "Great Ditch" forever tied New York City (via the Hudson River) to the Great Lakes.

A portrait of DeWitt Clinton by Rembrandt Peale (1823). *Public domain.*

In opening the American Midwest as far as Chicago (with its cattle and wheat/corn) and Minnesota (with its timber and ores) and the South (with its sugar and cotton), the heart of the North American continent (dubbed the "Inland Empire") was linked to the "Empire City." The crossroads of the colonies was now the entrepôt to the continent. It would remain so until well into the mid-twentieth century. The workshop and port of the nation were now at Clinton's (and our) community's doorstep.

Perhaps his most extraordinary legacy is a philosophy he held on life. Like a bottomless well, his words never seem to fail to quench our thirst for meaning. They define the spirit on which our national social ethic was founded: "Pleasure is a shadow, wealth is vanity, and power a pageant, but knowledge is ecstatic in enjoyment, perennial in fame, unlimited in space, and indefinite in duration."

Chapter 14

WHO WAS VERNON?

*E*benezer Stevens, born on August 11, 1751, in Roxbury, Massachusetts, died on September 2, 1823, in Rockaway, New York, and is buried in Astoria. He was a lieutenant colonel in the Continental army during the American Revolution, a major general in the New York state militia in the War of 1812 and a New York City merchant.

His training as an officer in the artillery gave him an unparalleled opportunity to be a more pivotal point of the Revolution than anyone, excepting perhaps only George Washington. His distinguished record included Bunker Bill, the British surrender at Saratoga and the war's end at the Siege of Yorktown. In addition, he served with distinction under Nathanael Greene, the Marquis de Lafayette and George Washington.

After fleeing from the Boston Tea Party, he found shelter with his friends Samuel and William Vernon, merchant bankers of Newport, Rhode Island, and leaders in the resistance to the taxation policy of Britain. He would never forget their kindness.

At war's end, Stevens moved to Astoria, purchasing much of the Hallett farm they had lost through their British support. He again witnessed history, as he was also one of the first to see the Treaty of Paris (ending the War of Independence) when it was delivered to New York, then the seat of government, by neighbor John Delafield.

The first decades of the nineteenth century were a time of rapid growth when, within a few decades, farmland transformed into blocks and lots and

Beers Atlas of Long Island, map of Long Island City (1873). *Greater Astoria Historical Society*

meandering country lanes turned into straight bullet turnpikes directly linking communities. In the budding neighborhood of Ravenswood, at Stevens's farm, he plotted streets named for Revolutionary leaders: Warren, Hancock, Hamilton, Washington, Marion, Jay and, as a tribute toward his friends at the beginning of his career, Vernon.

The Ravenswood, Hallett's Point and Williamsburgh Turnpike Road & Bridge Company, with the backing of Astoria's Stephan Halsey, was chartered in 1838 to connect the Village of Astoria with the City of Williamsburgh in Kings County. It built the first bridge over Newtown Creek, linking Hunters Point to Greenpoint. Unfortunately, until the charter expired in 1868, the tollhouse at either end was entitled to a fee derived from a somewhat overly detailed charter that described a fee structure base on a dizzying array of conveyances and types of traffic (animal or human). It never seemed to be well run or make a profit. Still, it did cement an essential link between Astoria and Brooklyn to a family whose identity is all but forgotten. It ran along the right of way dubbed on old maps as "Vernon Boulevard," its name today.

Chapter 15

CITIZEN OF THE WORLD

*A*n essayist once said that Pennsylvania produced two great leaders: Benjamin Franklin and Albert Gallatin. Both held prominent roles in the early years of our republic. They were successful entrepreneurs with interests in science, literature and education and were respected by those who knew them. Both would fit seamlessly within our modern times.

Franklin's adopted hometown, Philadelphia, honors him. Gallatin's adopted hometown, Astoria, knows nothing of him.

Gallatin, a student of the Enlightenment, believed that when human nature was free from social restrictions, it would display noble qualities. The democratic spirit of the new American Republic in the late 1780s attracted him, and he decided to emigrate from his birthplace, Geneva, Switzerland, to New England.

He soon moved to the American frontier, at that time western Pennsylvania, and with inheritance established a community, Friendship Hill. He rapidly rose to local prominence and was elected to the committee in Philadelphia, the seat of government, to help draft the Bill of Rights. Then, in 1799, Gallatin was elected to the House of Representatives. He became the de facto leader of the House Democrats a year later. It was a position that enabled him to aid his political ally Thomas Jefferson in winning the presidency.

Gallatin was rewarded with an appointment to the secretary of the treasury. He held this office for fifteen years—the longest tenure of anyone with that responsibility. His performance was outstanding. He paid off a good portion of the Revolutionary War debt, provided funding for the

Albert Gallatin statue. U.S. Department of Treasury headquarters, Washington, D.C. *Benoît Prieur—CC-BY-SA 2012.*

Louisiana Purchase, supported the National Bank (which gave stability to the infant republic's banking system) and funded a network of turnpikes that knit the young republic together.

His next role, as ambassador to both France and then England, was equally stellar. He helped negotiate the Treaty of Ghent, ending the War of 1812, and established an Anglo-American partnership over the administration of Oregon Territory.

Gallatin believed that one's future should be determined by merit. After retiring from public life in 1830, he sponsored a three-day conference in New York City attended by prominent merchants, bankers and traders. The object was to design an institution of higher learning for those "who would be admitted based upon ability rather than birthright or social class." New York University was the product of this discussion. He was elected its first president. His final accomplishment was to found the American Ethnological Society in 1842, the oldest organization in the United States to support anthropological research on human cultures.

On August 12, 1849, Gallatin died in his daughter's arms at home in the Village of Astoria, near Halletts Cove. He was eighty-eight.

There are seven towns, seven roads, six schools, five counties, one national forest, one river, one mountain range and one airport named in his honor. His face appeared on currency and postage stamps. Gallatin Bank was one of the parent institutions of today's Chase JP Morgan Bank. His memory remains strong within the Department of the Treasury. Several revenue cutters (small lightly armed boats used to enforce regulations and catch smugglers) bore his name. His statue is in front of the Treasury Building. The Albert Gallatin Award is the treasury's highest honorary career service award.

Despite this record of lifetime accomplishment, Gallatin, a member of the Democratic Party and native French speaker, was attacked by opponents (then the Federalist Party, today known as the Republican Party) for his foreign accent.

A biographical sketch by a grandson, John Austin Stevens, paints a fitting tribute to this remarkable man:

> *His moral excellence was no less conspicuous than his intellectual power. He had a profound sense of justice, a love of liberty, and an unfaltering belief in the human race's capacity for self-rule. Versed in the learning of centuries and familiar with every government experiment, he was full of the liberal spirit of his age. To a higher degree than any American, native or foreign-born, unless Franklin, with whose broad nature he had many traits in common, Albert Gallatin deserves the proud title, aimed at by many, reached by few—Citizen of the World.*

Chapter 16

OUR LADY OF MOUNT CARMEL

*I*n 1839, when a group of petitioners, led by Stephen Halsey, finally convinced Albany to grant a charter to the newly minted Village of Astoria, their work had just begun. First, there were streets to be laid out, and highways to other villages had to cross over marsh and farms. Next, store owners and craftsmen had to be convinced to move out to the country. Then, infrastructure (such as a village dock) had to be built. Finally, commercial activity had to be set up to cement the budding community's economic base.

The village was fortunate in its inception. There was a ready supply of laborers to build its docks and highways, clerk its stores, police its streets and be the maids and groundskeepers for the lawyers and bankers who owned the waterfront and hilltop estates.

The 1840s was the time of the Great Famine in Ireland. More than a few of the thousands who came to America found their way to the Village of Astoria. That is how Margaret Kelly, Rose Murphy, Bridget Christy, Rose Muldarry and dozens of others came to be buried in Astoria's Irish Famine Cemetery.

The prime waterfront real estate was set aside for the rich—and industry. The immigrant Irish could find only small plots east of Main Avenue and 18th Street. Here, on marginal land next to a swampy area, they built small cottages. Nearby was a gate along the side of the road (today Newtown Avenue) that colonists built to give cattle access to the marsh's salt grass.

Irish Famine Cemetery (1840s–1920s) on 21st Street, Astoria. *Greater Astoria Historical Society.*

When they went to work at McAloney's Carpet Factory, the Irish had to go through the gate and walk along a path that soon became a road. As a tribute to the Irish, everyone called it Emerald Street. It was no accident that it was on Emerald Street that the Irish built their first community—and their church with its cemetery. Today, Emerald Street is 21st Street and remains a vital thoroughfare within the community.

As early as 1835, Reverend Michael Curran, pastor of St. Paul's Roman Catholic Church in Harlem, took the Hell Gate Ferry to Hallets Cove (as Astoria Village was then known) to conduct mass at the home of a Mr. Tobin. The congregation grew in due time, and a parish, Our Lady of Mount Carmel, was organized on August 20, 1840. It was the first—or by some accounts the second—Roman Catholic parish in Queens. A small frame building near 26th Avenue and 21st Street was dedicated on July 10, 1842. Halsey, a Presbyterian, donated the stone for its foundation. The land itself was gifted by both Catholics and Protestants. The earliest recorded burial was in 1844.

The congregation continued to expand. After the Civil War, it became increasingly apparent that the building and its tiny cemetery—crammed on a lot that was only 82 by 188 feet—was hopelessly inadequate. In 1869, the congregation began a campaign to raise money for a new church that was to be built a few blocks east on Crescent Street. It was dedicated on August 17, 1873.

The old location was used for a few years as a Sunday school until the need for burial space became acute, and the building was torn down. The cemetery holds at least 150 burials and, with one exception (an Italian gardener who maintained the grounds), is exclusively Irish. In addition, it is the final resting place for nine Civil War veterans. The last interment was in 1926. Over the years, the cemetery was vandalized, cleaned up and then promptly forgotten. Finally, in 1983, the Diocese of Brooklyn took over its maintenance, picked up the toppled stones and enclosed the area in a secure fence. As a result, at least a tiny fragment of Old Astoria Village will be saved.

The tombstones face east—to Ireland.

Chapter 17

RESPECTABLE, TEMPERATE MEN

*I*t is a mystery why, unlike the other regions around New York, Queens has few original accounts of its early years. Lazy doodles on the margins of seventeenth-century town minutes betray a clerk's boredom. An astute eighteenth-century traveler records the pace of village and farm life for perhaps a season in a letter to a friend before moving on. A run of an early nineteenth-century newspaper of a few months slams shut a door to the past almost as quickly as it opens. Someone found a diary with entries such as "Today I exchanged greeting with Halsey on the street."

But there are rare cracks of light in the darkness, such as this October 1, 1866 vignette titled "A Little Sketch of What Astoria Was Twenty-Five Years Ago." It places us at a vantage point of about 1840, a few years after Astoria's founding. It was written by storekeeper Edwin Mills, who was involved in early civic affairs of the community.

His narrative starts by mentioning two churches, Episcopal and Reformed (while ignoring the third, a Roman Catholic parish), which had doubled in size during those first decades, a period when a few dozen homes had grown to a community of about four hundred souls. But, as is typical of New York to this day, the population was not stable; mills could count but a half dozen residents living in the same homes throughout a generation.

His account mentioned that Manhattan's 3rd Avenue with a right turn at East 86th Street were roads in "splendid traveling condition" and was the favored route to the Astoria Ferry (the Manhattan name for the Hell Gate Ferry).

Men in New York, circa 1840. *Mathew Brady, Library of Congress.*

He continues: "The Hell Gate Ferry terminated at Flushing Avenue [Astoria Boulevard], which was also the point of departure for the primary road on Long Island's North Shore" (now Route 25A beyond Flushing). Heavily traveled then (as it is today), "it was not uncommon to see ten or twenty hay and market wagons from Flushing and points east patiently waiting for their turn to cross to Manhattan on the ferry."

Mills painted a vivid picture of Astoria evenings during those first years: "At the ferry stood two rival hotels, each founded by a ship captain. Both were well kept and did a prosperous business. It was customary for many of Astoria's best citizens, middle-aged and older, to spend a portion of almost every evening at one of the hotels. There they played a few games of dominoes and had one or more of their celebrated brandy punches." Described as "respectable temperate men," they went home. They spent the balance of their evening with their families.

"On Christmas and New Year's eves," Mills continued, "they invariably had a raffle for poultry, would stay a little later, and indulge a little more freely. This custom rendered the hotels more respectable, better kept, more quiet and orderly, and kept boys from frequenting them; in fact, boys at that time had not got the idea that hotels, strong drink, and cigars were meant expressly for them."

PART II

Village of Astoria:
Long Island City
(1840–1898)

Chapter 18

ROADS STREWN WITH FLOWERS

*T*he technology of cyberspace and social media has unleashed a flood of information between us that is so pervasive—and casual—that it is nearly incomprehensible to those not of a certain age to understand. Not too long ago, even with the telephone, television, newspaper, book and letter correspondence, information was scant, expensive and often incomplete. As a result, there is almost no firsthand account of our community's early years. Sure, there are records of street paving, officeholders and the price of beans in the local shop, but what was life like, and how did it feel?

Therefore, consider the account of a local nurseryman, Grant Thorburn, of a Sunday afternoon ride from Manhattan out to the rural suburbs of Queens—say an imaginary narrative of a young couple out on an afternoon date in the 1840s with a rented carriage and a spirited trotter. This would have set the young man back about $1 (about $120 in today's wages). It was his disposable income for that week.

At that time, Manhattanites lived between Canal and 14th Streets. After renting a one-horse shay for an afternoon, armed with a packed picnic basket and picking the young lady up at her home, they would cross the East River on the Peck Slip Ferry. Conveyed to the Grand Street terminal in Williamsburg, they would turn the horse to the northeast. Keeping the river to their left, they continued on the newly opened "smooth, quiet, and beautiful" Ravenswood, Halletts Cove and Williamsburg Turnpike (today Manhattan Avenue in Brooklyn and Vernon Boulevard in Queens). Around them, "thriving" farms cultivated by German families seemed frozen in time.

A couple in a sulky with fields of flowers. *Public domain.*

This enabled them to reach Astoria within forty minutes. After crossing the Newtown Creek Bridge, the next quarter mile was a treat with the whimsical and exuberant mansions of the Ravenswood nouveau riche. Finally, crossing over the tide mill bridge that dammed Sunswick Creek (the curve in Vernon Boulevard at the north edge of Socrates Park), they would come to Thorburn's Gardens (31st Drive). Here "among plants domestic and exotic, everyone has a clean shirt and is sober," as Thorburn said of his employees, who stood ready to assist in that right purchase for "m'lady's garden."

Thorburn's narrative continues: "After your purchase and perhaps a lunch beside the green-houses of dahlias, and sensitive plants," our party continued north, which brought them "straight through the main street of Astoria; from then lies before you a new, level, straight, and beautiful road to Flushing toll-gate" (Astoria Boulevard). Cautioning them not to enter for it "will cost you four or five shillings," the account suggests you "tack about just this side of the toll-gate, keep a southwest course—it's a fine road [Hazen Street]—and an hour's easy drive [Woodside Avenue and then Broadway] will bring you up at the Dutch Church in Newtown [Elmhurst]. Then on to the good road [Grand Avenue] back to Williamsburg and the ferry to Manhattan."

In the writer's mind, there was no comparison between an afternoon's ride in Queens and that in Manhattan: "The roads which I have described [in Queens] are now literally strewed with flowers from the cherry, peach, and apple-trees with which they are lined. How much more sociable, comfortable and reasonable is a drive on these roads than going up the Third Avenue to Harlem, where you encounter meat-carts, dirt-carts, brick-carts, and hog-carts, with wild horses driven by savage men. You may drive seven miles without even meeting a sober-sided old Dutch wagon."

Chapter 19

THE (ASTORIA?) COCKTAIL

*H*as not food and drink always found a special place in Astoria? Our community has always, it seems, had a range of both dining and drinking opportunities of which most other places could only dream.

For example, Bohemian Hall and Beer Garden has been serving Pilsner Urquell, the first pilsner on the face of the earth, for more than a century—even surviving Prohibition! This place still offers a simple recipe: a cold beer with good friends on a hot night. This treasure shaped a new generation to discover and enjoy the leisure ways of a past generation.

Who would guess that even earlier, when it was yet farmland, our community played a significant role in American agriculture? Gentleman farmers, tinkering with genetics in the long-gone hothouses and orchards of Ravenswood, were pivotal in developing both the California wine and the Washington apple industries. But these are stories for another time.

A rumor circulates through the community from time to time: it is claimed that the Manhattan cocktail was developed in Old Astoria Village. The story states that, as their vessels waited for the tide's turn at Hell Gate, farmers and tradesmen would while their time at a tavern that stood near the old ferry on Main Avenue in Old Astoria. The legend has the barkeep concocting a new drink for them. They dubbed it the "Manhattan Cocktail."

Is this true?

Various references are of little help. They state that the drink has "several stories behind its invention." Its Wikipedia entry examines a number of

A watercolor of boats awaiting tide at Hell Gate, circa 1890. *Greater Astoria Historical Society.*

these theories. The most popular story states that the cocktail started with "a drink at New York's Manhattan Club in the early 1870s…invented for a banquet hosted by Lady Randolph Churchill (mother of Winston Churchill) to honor presidential candidate Samuel Tilden."

Wiki also cites references that go back further in time, including that of a bartender named Black who invented it at a "bar on Broadway near Houston Street" in the 1860s.

Despite its murky past, the drink has clearly remained popular over time. One recent mixologist described it as "the perfect drink for both a strong man and a smooth woman."

For boatmen, time was money, and they knew tide tables intimately. Their arrival at Hell Gate would have been timed to be within minutes of the good tides they wanted; the passage was quickly filled with ships ready to slip through at the change of tide. It was not a fleet wallowing at anchor, with everyone ashore drinking and their unguarded boats, full of goods, an easy mark for a thief.

Besides, who would face the dangerous Hell Gate impaired by a beverage? Only a fool.

Chapter 20

THE HUNTERS
OF HUNTERS POINT

ong Island City comprises many communities: Astoria, Sunnyside, Ravenswood, Dutch Kills, Steinway, Old Astoria Village and Hunters Point. This installment discusses the family behind the heart of our fair city, the Hunters of Hunters Point.

The political and administrative heart of Long Island City has always been "downtown," the junction of Vernon and Jackson Avenues, and the surrounding territory termed Hunters Point on old maps. It is difficult for us to realize that as recently as 1850, this area was a small island bisected by Vernon Avenue and hardly more than four blocks wide and a little less than that in length. The rest of Hunters Point was a vast meadow, low-lying and flooded at every tide by the waters of the East River.

On November 30, 1900, the *Long Island Star-Journal* ran an interview with "an old-timer from the neighborhood," sixty-four-year-old Jacob B. Hunter, at his home on Hunter Street. The portrait included in this chapter is of his father, Jacob Hunter (1791–1875).

> *"Young man,"* said Mr. Hunter, *"I want to tell you about Hunter's Point* [editor's note: old style with the apostrophe]. *As I first knew it, the place was the prettiest spot in all New York State. Perhaps you don't believe that, and I don't blame you very much, considering present appearances, but it is true just the same. There weren't any smokestacks to belch out smoke along this part of the river.*

"I can remember when Newtown Creek was a pretty and clear stream, and not marred by factories and filled with grease and oil. And do you know I used to catch out of that creek all the fish and soft shell crabs the whole family could eat? It wouldn't take me more than half an hour to get a big catch.

"My father and I used to row across Newtown Creek and walk along the river bank to Williamsburg, where we would take the Grand Street ferry and go over to Barnum's Museum. It was down on the corner of Fulton Street and Broadway then, and a right interesting place it was for us boys too. There were all sorts of curiosities and animals. They had a sort of vaudeville entertainment, too. It beats your swell theaters, let me tell you!"

Hunter explained that in the 1850s, the view of the city from Hunters Point was not very good, as the building of Manhattan had not spread much above 23rd Street. "Herald Square was a waste of rocky land, and what is now Central Park was about the dirtiest place I ever saw." He elaborated, "It was a sort of cow and pig pasture combined."

The age-old character of Hunters Point as a low island above tidewater came to an end with the death of Jacob's grandparents Captain George Hunter and his wife, Ann. The widow provided in her will that her three sons, Jacob, John and Richard, should sell off Hunters Point within three years after her death. On June 17, 1835, the estate was sold for $100,000. Jacob's family moved to a farm on 29th Street in Dutch Kills. By 1900,

Jacob Hunter, from *History of Queens County*, W.W. Munsell (1882). *Public domain.*

the time of Jacob's interview, the ancestral home was long gone; the sand from its hill had been used to fill in the marshy riverbank. A good portion of his Dutch Kills farm had also disappeared under Queens Plaza.

On April 15, 1916, sixteen years after this interview, Jacob Bennett Hunter passed away, the last member of the family living in the community. Hunter Street was named for his family.

Chapter 21

THE FATHER OF
LONG ISLAND CITY

*E*veryone is a historian; the very fabric of our lives contributes to the substance of our community's narrative. Every page from our past is mirrored around us. We simply need to look about with this fresh perception, and there it is—in plain sight!

Long Island City is being transformed into a great community that echoes the dreams of a forgotten past. But this promise lacks genuine authenticity without something faithful from that time. Perhaps the first step is to replace byways with drab names (11th Street, 47th Avenue and 47th Road) with names they once had (Ely, Van Alst and Hunter). These are names of real meaning. Over time, we will examine them. We start today with Henry Sheldon Anable, namesake of Anable Basin and formerly 48th Avenue.

Henry Sheldon Anable, who died in 1883, was one of the oldest and best-known residents in the community. He was once called by some the "Father of Long Island City." Most of his contemporaries credited him as the driving force that shaped and pushed the community forward and converted it from farmland to an urban center in the years before incorporation.

He was born at a very fortunate time, 1815, when the country was finally at peace. His birthplace, Albany, had a front window to the Erie Canal, which opened during the decade of his birth. The waterway threw a large section of the Midwest open for development by linking the Great Lakes and Mississippi Valley to New York and Atlantic destinations. It was a perfect place for a young man of ambition.

Henry built a successful dry goods business between New York and the Midwest. His offices were in Utica, New York, and Sheboygan, Wisconsin. In 1852, while in his mid-thirties, he traveled to Sacramento, California, looking for business opportunities. Years later, he recalled traveling in a "prairie schooner," a wagon drawn by teams of mules seen in iconic images of the time or period westerns.

In 1855, when a group of investors and the trustees of Union College (which then owned most of Hunters Point) sought someone to improve their property, Henry was an ideal choice. He was to spend the next thirty years, the balance of his life, as both agent and property manager, developing the heart of our community.

Henry Sheldon Anable, from *History of Queens County*, W.W. Munsell (1882). *Public domain.*

He built Jackson Avenue, the first significant road within Hunters Point. Then, Anable surfaced Thomson Avenue, which was the grandest boulevard in the county and the most critical factor in opening up the last undeveloped area called Long Island City Heights (Sunnyside). Renamed Queens Boulevard, it was later extended to the then rural sections of central and southern Queens.

He docked the waterfront, filled in the swamps, cut the hills and laid out a system of streets and avenues. This man deserves credit for inducing both the Flushing and the Long Island Rail Roads to build their terminals at the East River waterfront. Disembarking passengers were transferred to another of his enterprises, the East River Ferry Company. Anable inaugurated a ferry service to Manhattan.

Anable was described as "influential and indefatigable" by a contemporary biographer. His peers recognized him as the person most responsible for securing a charter for the city and moving the Queens County seat (which then also included Nassau County) to Long Island City.

In the new city administration, Anable served at various posts and completed most of the work he had started a generation before. He transformed a muddy, raw rail town into the most dynamic community on Long Island.

Over the years, Union College entrusted him with $250,000 (by some measures, as much as a half billion dollars in today's currency). His books accounted for every penny.

Chapter 22

STREET NAME ROLL CALL

*E*ly Avenue was named for Charles Ely, a native of West Springfield, Massachusetts, and Yale graduate (class of 1825). He moved to New York City in the 1840s and opened up the dry goods firm of Merritt, Ely & Co. Ely was one of the charter trustees of the Mutual Life Insurance Company of New York, known today as MONY.

Mutual of New York was a pioneer in the insurance industry. It helped develop mortality tables, actuarial techniques and premium computations, and from its flow of cash from insurance premiums, it was a heavy investor in government securities, state bonds and—figuring into our story—real estate mortgages. The developers of Hunters Point, Union College, must have needed Ely because of his access to the insurance company's supply of cash. The acquisition of farms, the grading and leveling of plots and streets and the building of houses took far more capital than college tuitions and endowments could ever hope to offer.

A glance at an old map shows Ely Avenue running north from Jackson Avenue. To the south of Jackson were A, B, C, D and E Streets, which later were named Arch, Beech, Crane, Davis and Pearson Streets. Nothing can be found on the naming of Arch or Beech (perhaps they were inspired by features on the Union College campus); other streets were named for people who participated in the early development of the Hunters Point community.

Crane Street is named for Ely's partner, Jonathan Crane (born 1789). Both Ely and Crane were deeply involved—perhaps as trustees—with Union College and its ambitious scheme to turn a city out of marsh and farm. Both of their sons were also graduates of the school. Ely's son, like his father, was also involved in land purchases on behalf of the college.

After Union College started to acquire land in Hunters Point, Ely and Crane took an active role in the community's development. Crane moved to Greenpoint and soon cleared the Griffin Farm (1850) and the Hunter Farm (1852). This land later became Blissville and the western portion of Hunters Point. About this time, the first streets were staked. By 1853, the two were filling water lots at the mouth of Newtown Creek.

Jonathan Pearson, from *History of Queens County*, W.W. Munsell (1882). *Public domain.*

Another momentous event of the 1850s was the doubling of the land area of Hunters Point. Between 1852 and 1858, the Van Alst Farm was acquired in stages; this great tract covered all the land from 21st Street to Dutch Kills Creek and from about 43rd Avenue south to Newtown Creek—in other words, the eastern half of today's Hunters Point. John G. Van Alst died in 1851, and his children conveyed to Messrs. Crane and Ely 131 acres of land for the sum of $50,000 in May 1853. Crane and Ely deeded one-third of the premises to Union College in February 1857, while the other two-thirds went to Leicester K. Ely (Charles Ely's son), William Judson and, ultimately, to Union College in 1860.

Crane, through marriage, was related to the Winans family. They were instrumental in the development of railroads in the country. It was the Winans who brought the railroad to Hunters Point and, by doing so, made the community viable—but this is a story for another time.

Davis Street is named for Dr. Job Davis, a doctor from Greenpoint, who put up the first buildings in Hunters Point with Crane in 1854. They were four-story brick buildings located on the north side of Borden Avenue, about two hundred feet east of Vernon Avenue.

Finally, Pearson Street is named for Jonathan Pearson, a Union College graduate who later became a professor at the institution and served as its treasurer for many decades. As a young man, he left a diary that recorded his trip on the Erie Canal in 1833. Unfortunately, of all the men profiled in this piece, only Pearson's portrait was found.

Chapter 23

THE FAMILY WHO OWNED QUEENS PLAZA

illiam Payntar, born in 1731, married Hester Skillman in 1764. As was customary for their time, the Payntars had large families and intermarried with their neighbors. With names like Skillman, Brinckerhoff, Wyckoff, Bragraw, Rapalye, Van Pelt and Debevoise, their family tree resembled a veritable index of Queens streets found in an old Hagstrom atlas of Long Island City.

The Payntars married well, for William received property that later became Queens Plaza from his wife's family in 1778. Their holdings extended from the Sunnyside Yards to Long Island City High School, including across Northern Boulevard from the present Clock Tower Building, Burger Jorissen's former mid-seventeenth-century Tide Mill (see chapter 3). Although the Erie Canal opened the Midwest wheat fields to the markets in the East, by the mid-1800s, the milling industry was almost obsolete in Long Island City.

Fortune changed for the Payntars in 1858. The Hunters Point, Newtown and Flushing Turnpike Road Company (Northern Boulevard) connected Long Island City, and Flushing was plotted through their farm. Two years later, the Long Island Rail Road laid track for their main line, paralleling the turnpike just a few hundred feet to the east. No longer needed, the tide mill gave way to the Long Island Rail Road when it cut through the marsh. The millstones, now relics of the past industry, were placed next to their home on the turnpike. Less than a mile to the south were Long Island City and the city of Brooklyn. Urban development was at their doorstep.

The generation that finally cut up the old farm was led by George Payntar, a former wholesale dry goods merchant who went into real estate. In 1867,

The Payntar family farmhouse, formerly Miller's House at Dutch Kills, circa 1700. *Greater Astoria Historical Society.*

at the age of thirty-three, he was busy plotting lots and streets through the upland acres just west of Northern Boulevard. George called his hamlet Payntarville. We call it Dutch Kills. The heart of the neighborhood, 40th Avenue, was once called Payntar Avenue.

In the window of Payntar's real estate office was a cannonball. The relic, found by cousin Howard Payntar on the family farm, was embedded in an old oak stump on the hill between Dutch Kills and Ravenswood. They told a story that it was fired by a British man-o'-war while Washington passed up the East River after the Battle of Long Island. However, a more likely explanation was that Americans in Manhattan fired it over the heads of the British crossing the East River during the Battle of Kips Bay.

Queens Plaza was once marshland where springs fed both Sunswick Creek, which ran along 21st Street, and Dutch Kills. Long Island City, dependent on wells or public pumps, lacked a decent local water supply. These springs on the Payntar farm were a potential solution to this crisis. In February 1869, the Payntarville Water Co. was incorporated, but nothing happened for reasons lost to history.

What to do with this unusable land? The solution came in 1901, when the marsh, the last undeveloped area on the East River, was chosen as the perfect location for Queens Plaza. Again, the Payntars received top dollar.

Only sixty-five feet north of Queens Plaza, the house somehow lingered through the wrenching changes brought to the area by Sunnyside Yards and

70

the Queensboro Bridge. It was sandwiched in a tiny ravine between one of the largest rail yards in the world and Northern Boulevard. Without any modern amenities such as running water or sewers, the ancient dwelling was uninhabitable. Kids from nearby Long Island City High School kept breaking into it and starting fires. One of George's sons, Elmer Payntar, finally put the 250-year-old landmark out of its misery by tearing it down and replacing it with an office building.

Chapter 24

SISTERS OF ST. JOSEPH

n 1861, Bishop Loughlin, head of the Catholic Diocese of Brooklyn, bought several small dwellings and twenty-nine lots fronting on Jackson Avenue, 44th Drive and 45th Avenue. He turned these over to the Sisters of St. Joseph to build a hospital—the first in Queens County. It took only a few months for local men, volunteering their labor, to convert the buildings into both a hospital and convent for the sisters. Tradition holds that Sister Mary David, one of the nuns charged with opening the facility, had fifty cents in liquid assets when she opened the hospital.

The first patient was Ann Schulster of Astoria, who had a fractured tibia. On June 4, 1897, the first baby born in the hospital, John Setti, was registered as "Saint John Setti" at the nuns' request on the hospital staff.

The years passed, and the population grew. The old wooden buildings became hopelessly inadequate. Finally, on January 7, 1900, the new St. John's Hospital at Jackson Avenue in Hunters Point was formally opened. Bishop Charles E. McDonnell delivered the blessing. The local paper, the *Long Island Star*, wrote:

> *The formal opening was…one of the most intensely impressive events in the history, not alone of the community in which the noble edifice has been raised, but also of the entire Borough of Queens and the whole of Long Island. The hospital is the culmination of years of arduous labor and earnest, persistent devotion on the part of the Sisters of St. Joseph, led by that grand woman, the sister superior in charge, Sister Mary David.*

St. John's Hospital on Jackson Avenue, postcard, circa 1900. *Greater Astoria Historical Society.*

Long before the hour for opening the doors of the new hospital, immense throngs gathered in front of the building, blocking thoroughfares for some distance. A parade featuring about one thousand marchers proceeded up Jackson Avenue to the hospital. Finally, at precisely 3:30 p.m., the doors of St. John's were thrown open, and the parade, preceded by police officers, marched into the building.

Those in the waiting crowd followed until, in the words of the *Star* reporter, "every passageway was filled and vantage-ground secured from which to view the ceremonies, which consisted of Bishop McDonnell and a small procession walking through every portion of the building, while blessing and consecrating it forever to the work of the Lord."

The hospital's interior consisted mainly of five floors of wards, but there were twenty-two private rooms. While patients could be admitted immediately, the facility would not be fully operational until February. Accounts of the opening day noted that the new facility could accommodate emergency cases of insanity. Two rooms in the basement had been set aside for "lunatics" (a medical term no longer in use but at the time used mainly for females) who were awaiting examination. The only other facility available for this was the county jail.

The hospital remained in Long Island City until 1961, when, as was the case sixty years before, the building could no longer meet the demands of new technologies. The board of trustees decided relocation was more efficient than renovation and purchased Horace Harding Hospital at 90–02 Queens Boulevard in Elmhurst and moved the hospital to that location. For a few decades, the old building was used as a dormitory and teaching pavilion for nurses. However, it had been torn down by the 1980s, when Citicorp built a tower at the hospital's former location. At midnight on March 1, 2009, St. John's Queens Hospital on Queens Boulevard closed its doors.

Chapter 25

QUEENS OF HEARTS

*L*ola Montez was once described by a biographer as "beautiful, intelligent, and courageous, yet egocentric and manipulative…and ahead of her time." Toward the end of her life, a chance encounter with an old friend, Marie Buchanan of Astoria, provided her with comfort and escape from the indignity of a likely Potters Field grave.

Lola Montez, Irish born in 1821 and christened Maria Dolores Eliza Rosanna Gilbert (Montez was a stage name; she had no Spanish ancestry), was the child of a soldier and the illegitimate daughter of a nobleman. She was taken to India as a child by her parents, and her father soon died and her mother remarried. By 1826, she had been sent to a boarding school in Scotland. Lola would have several brief marriages but was childless.

You must exercise as a wild and romping spirited girl who runs up and down as if her veins were full of wine.

After taking dancing lessons and making a stage debut in London, she invented a new name and backstory: Lola Montez, "artistic" dancer. Then, liberating herself from the social conventions of her time, she moved to Continental Europe. Lola was soon a legend in a century noted for its outsized adventurers—by taking up with, in short order, composer Franz Liszt, novelist Alexandre Dumas and finally, the greatest prize, King Ludwig I of Bavaria.

Lola Montez, profile with black veil (1853). *Thomas Easterly Daguerreotype Collection, Missouri Historical Society, Wikimedia.*

Be not afraid of yourself, trust your soul—dare to stand in the might of your individuality to meet the tidal currents of the world.

Within a remarkably short time, the king made her the countess of Landsfeld, gave her a large annuity and all but ceded to her control the governing of five million Bavarians. As she dismissed the prime minister and sponsored legislation supporting students and working people, her actions angered the conservative elite, tore the country apart and triggered a revolution. The disgraced king abdicated. Lola fled the country (with her jewels, of course).

I have never claimed to be famous. Notorious I have always been.

She returned to the stage with a new act and, to silence hecklers, supplemented her act with cracking a whip on stage. Playing a sultry vamp, she traveled across America (1851) to the goldfields of California (1853), the mining camps of Australia (1855) and finally back to Europe in triumph (1857). At that time, no woman had traveled those distances. A photograph of her holding a cigarette is regarded as the earliest image of a woman smoking.

I have known all that the world has to give—all!

She transformed into another act: a serious orator and author who lectured on style, fashion and gossip. Her lectures demonstrated that she was educated and well read. But photos and critics commented that she was aging rapidly. The public did not know that she was both penniless and gripped at the advanced stages of illness. A chance encounter on a sidewalk in Chelsea reunited Lola with her childhood friend Marie Buchanan of Astoria.

I am tired.
—last words of Lola Montez

A sudden stroke, which all but incapacitated her, made international news. She spent her final months with the Buchanans in residence at the extensive gardens of their Astoria flower nursery on Newtown Road and Buchanan (today 29th) Street. After she passed away, the Buchanans hosted her well-attended funeral at their home, paid for her burial plot and stone and inscribed it with her birth name: Eliza Gilbert (1811–1861). Warren Buchanan, a great-great-grandson of Marie Buchanan, recalled that "as late as the 1950s we toasted Montez by drinking Bloody Marys at her grave." Her fans have made that grave in Greenwood Cemetery, Brooklyn, a place of pilgrimage from around the world.

Feel the fire where she walks, Lola Montez so beautiful, Oh Lola I'm sure
that love, would be the key to all your pains.
—from "Lola Montez" by Danish heavy metal group Volbeat

A standard played before thousands of ecstatic fans at all Volbeat concerts, "Lola Montez" is from the band's gold *Outlaw Gentlemen and Shady Ladies* (2013) album. Ageless Lola, 160 years after she was laid to rest, still connects to a new generation.

Chapter 26

COAT OF ARMS

*I*n 1870, naval engineer Benjamin Maillefert, who gained fame for removing some of the rocks at the Hell Gate, recalled how the name "Long Island City" came about:

> *The honor of giving to "Long Island City" its name…belongs to Capt. Levy Hayden, late superintendent of the Marine railway [gantries] at Hunter's Point. About 1853, a member of the Beebe family of Ravenswood took many shares in the railway's stock; and inquired what name should be given to the concern and the surrounding country, which was perfectly wild. The captain thought that Hunter's Point, Ravenswood, and Astoria would soon become a large city; therefore, he suggested the name "Long Island City" for the place. An immense flag was at once hoisted on the building with the name written in full.*

The Common Council of Long Island City in 1873 adopted the coat of arms as "emblematical of the varied interests represented by Long Island City." It was designed by George Williams of Ravenswood. But unfortunately, no further details were given to attach meaning to its elements that are heraldic and mementos from our past.

For example, the canoe recalls our key location within the network of waterways established before European settlement; the tomahawk is our first manufactured item, crafted by Hendrick Harmenson of Bowery Bay 350 years ago. Windmill arms symbolize the wind and tidal mills that dotted our

The coat of arms of Long Island City is embedded with the website address of the Greater Astoria Historical Society. *Greater Astoria Historical Society.*

landscape. The anchor recalls the industry that lined the waterfront along the East River, Newtown Creek and Dutch Kills. Beehives are traditional symbols of hard work and industry.

Minerva, the Roman goddess of crafts and trade guilds, holds a pole topped by a Phrygian cap traditionally given to freed slaves. It symbolizes the grassroots overthrow of the old political order in Queens with the creation of Long Island City. She is also associated with spinning (weaving was important throughout our history) and was the inventor of musical instruments (harking the role of instrument makers Steinway, Sohmer and Gemunder).

Bearded Neptune, holding the trident (the three-pointed spear) that was used in myth to shatter stone, recalls the city's efforts to blast Hell Gate reefs. As the creator of horses and patron of horse races, Neptune's prominent position on the shield recalls when crowds went to the horse racetracks that once dotted the landscape of Queens, underpinning much of the commercial activity in the saloons and ferries at Hunters Point.

The Minerva and Neptune symbols have another dimension, for in their Greek incarnation as Athena and Poseidon, they recall a story of a competition they held over who would be the protector of Athens. Athena produced the olive and Poseidon the horse. As symbolized by the olive, the gods decided that agriculture was a more significant benefit to mankind—and consequently named the city of Athens after her. In Long Island City, highly profitable truck farms and greenhouses, which supplied Manhattan's voracious appetite, were far more important economically than "wagering on the ponies" by the sporting and drinking crowd.

Over the shield, the bald eagle is taken from the Village of Astoria coat of arms. The panels on each side depict waterfront industry, old Astoria Village and the railroads.

The version seen here, displayed with the web address of the Greater Astoria Historical Society, is the society's official logo.

Chapter 27

A SMALL GLADE OFF SHORE ROAD

A good historian develops a keen sense of time and thereby lives in a world of four, rather than three, dimensions. Take them to any location, and they can sense the present and an invisible timeline of people and places from the past.

For example, just north of the Hell Gate Bridge is a small glade just off Shore Road. It's an inviting pool of sunlight surrounded by a perimeter of trees. People loll about, working on their tans.

It was once the home of the Barclays. They were an old family of Scottish stock and first made their way into the annals of history as traders along the Baltic and Scandinavian coasts. One became a Russian prince who was the architect behind Napoleon's defeat in Russia; another became a partner of Barclays Bank, a significant player in today's financial markets. Closer to home, another Barclay, a Quaker, was close friends with William Penn and George Fox. For nearly a decade, he governed most of New Jersey from his home in England, three thousand miles away—no small feat in the seventeenth century.

Our story starts with Reverend Thomas Barclay, who, as the first Anglican rector of Albany, spread the Church of England faith to English, Dutch and Mohawk alike. One son, John Barclay, became the mayor of Albany. Another, Reverend Henry Barclay, followed in his father's footsteps and became the second rector of Trinity Church in Manhattan. (Yes, he is the person after whom Barclay Street is named.) Reverend Barclay was also one of the founders of Columbia University.

Barclay Mansion on Shore Road, postcard, circa 1890. *Greater Astoria Historical Society.*

Reverend Barclay's son, Major Thomas Barclay, was a member of New York's social elite. He owned a mansion near Hell Gate. During the American Revolution, he organized a Loyalist militia. When the British lost the colonies, he fled to Nova Scotia, where he rose to political prominence. The British government assigned him to New York City as British consul in 1799. Two of his sons became merchants and agents for Lloyds of London.

About 1840, some sixty years after Major Barclay abandoned his estate at the Hell Gate to flee to Canada, a nephew, Henry, returned to the area, purchased property and built a grand home. It was no longer the rural countryside but a smart new suburban retreat rebranded as Astoria, Long Island. Into that house, he brought his bride. There, his children and grandchildren were born, and it was there that he died. In the early years, the family recalled that one of the last of the Wards of Ward's Island used to pay a visit after crossing the Hell Gate on horseback.

One of Henry's sons, also named Henry, took over the house upon his father's death in 1863. Henry Jr. had no real job but was a millionaire nevertheless. He earned income from the Barclay Building in lower Manhattan, built on land his family had owned since the 1740s, a generation before the American Revolution.

In the parlance of the time, Henry was known as a "sportsman." On his twenty-first birthday, he joined the Union Club. He was a charter member of the Metropolitan Club and one of the founders of the Lambs Club. He was also a member of the Lenox, Southampton and Meadowbrook Country Clubs.

Henry Barclay bred both dogs and horses and was primarily responsible for developing the American trotting horse. His stables in Woodside once held 120 foals. He also owned an estate in Lenox, Massachusetts, where he bred horses, and at the time of his death, he was planning a larger breeding farm in New Jersey. Unfortunately, his heart gave out after taking his team out for exercise in Manhattan. He died the following afternoon—in yet another home on Washington Square North.

Although his obituary still listed Astoria, Long Island, among the Barclay residences, the family had drifted away from the manse years before. His daughters held their coming-out parties at family residences in Manhattan, and they spent long summers playing at the Long Island summer resorts

Therefore, no one was surprised that when Henry passed away in 1905, his youngest daughter, Clara, as executrix of the estate, offered the old house for sale to the Rickert-Finley Realty Corporation. The parcel was simply described as 125 lots. A few months later, the city announced the land would be part of a new Astoria park.

Chapter 28

THE STEINWAYS
LEAVE MANHATTAN

*D*uring the New York City Draft Riots in 1863, when the streets ruled the city for three terrifying days, a mob of thousands carrying torches and assorted weapons marched on the Steinway factory. Forewarned, armed workers stared back from factory windows. Payments in cash were made. Then, the horde slowly drifted away. It was only by chance that a torch was not tossed through an open window onto some sawdust or lacquer in a vat. If that had happened, the corner of Park Avenue and 54th Street soon would have become a brick-walled ruin. The story would have ended there.

Throughout the 1860s, things got much worse. Workforce loyalty was tested by wave after wave of anarchists, socialists and other assorted labor agitators who showed up repeatedly at the factory's front door trying to form unions or announce a work stoppage at a moment's notice in sympathy for another shop across town.

Adding to the family's woes, the Park Avenue factory quickly became a noose about their necks. After less than two decades, they had run out of room to expand. As a result, production fell behind a growing cascade of piano orders. Even worse, there was no place for log storage—an essential step in piano production. Wood, when cut, is "green" and must be first stacked to dry out or "season" for at least a year. The Steinways needed acres by the growing concern—not city lots.

William Steinway sent agents around the metropolitan area. He soon received reports of a "beautiful garden spot surrounded by wastelands and vacant lots" in the Astoria section of Long Island City, Queens. It was near

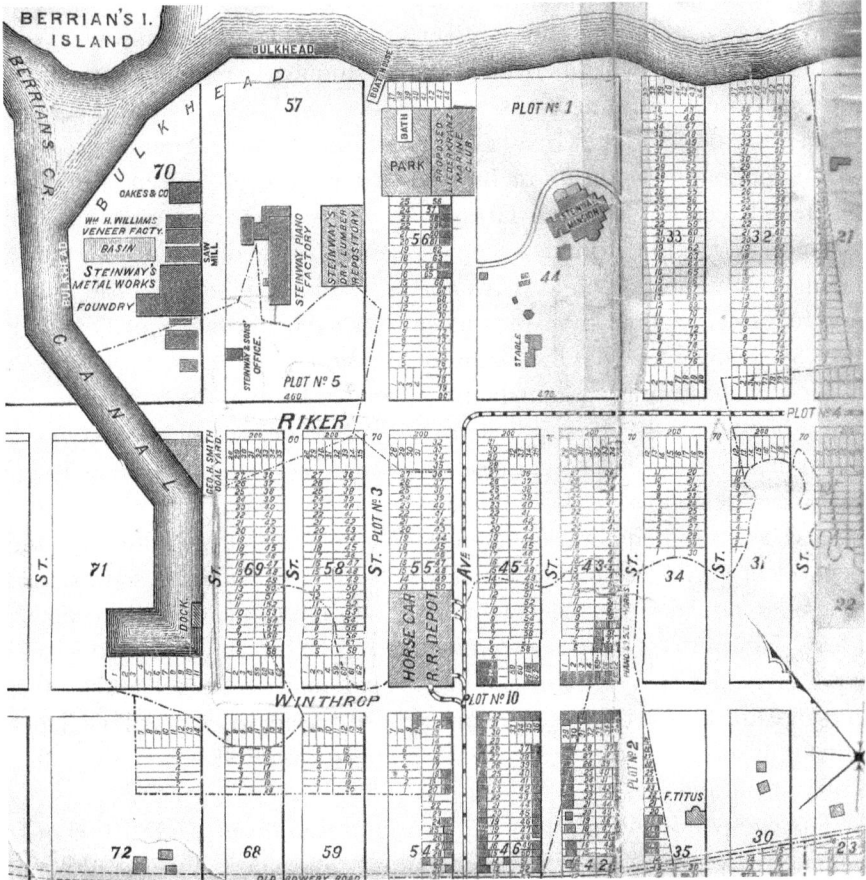

Map used by Steinway to sell the lot at the Steinway Settlement, circa 1870. *Henry Z. Steinway Collection, Greater Astoria Historical Society.*

Greater New York's geographical center, only five miles from New York City Hall. Even better, it had a half mile of waterfront that was perfect for both unloading bulk material as logs and future development.

Making no secret of Steinway's intentions, flush with cash (and perhaps goaded to move quickly by the Steinways), their agents offered premium prices. Naturally, the local farmers had no problem selling at that level. Ultimately, the company purchased some four hundred acres. For the next eighty years—as late as the 1950s—they were selling lots.

Before starting community building, the Steinways made a permanent record of their accomplishment by hauling a camera to the top of a tall building (perhaps the Wilson Nursery windmill that stood at what would be today's intersection of Steinway Street and Grand Central Parkway). They took six pictures and knitted them into a stunning panoramic view from the Hell Gate to Flushing Bay. Copies are displayed at the Steinway & Sons factory entrance and the Greater Astoria Historical Society museum.

It is undoubtedly the most breathtaking picture of Queens from the nineteenth century, showing farms with a few waterfront estates in the distance. In the foreground, a lane (20th Road) is lined with tidy farms of families with names such as Titus and Kouwenhoven, echoing the Dutch era. In the center, on a knoll, is a mansion owned by the family of Benjamin Pike. We know it today as the Steinway Mansion.

Most of the setting was marsh and vacant land, but to the Steinways, this was a blank canvas. They approached it as a composer would set about to fill an unscored page of sheet music. A symphony was about to be written.

William zealously set about building a utopian community, going about his task, as his contemporaries noted, with "a very liberal, philanthropic, and benevolent spirit." Although the Steinway Settlement had many enlightened amenities provided by the company, it was emphatically no "company town." Housing was open to everyone. Real estate brochures showed several types of model houses (many still in the community today). The map that accompanies this article was for prospective buyers to choose their block and lot. It showed a street grid already mapped with trolley lines, sidewalks, water mains and sewers.

The company built a public bathhouse, a waterfront park, a firehouse with apparatus served by a volunteer company and a post office. In addition, it donated land for churches and public schools. The community boasted one of the first kindergartens in the country. The Steinway Lending Library, through mergers, later became the Queens Library, which has the largest circulation in the country. A portrait of William Steinway remained in the system throughout the years and is now in the library's Steinway Branch.

Steinway Street was planned as a commercial district that served the community's needs. A bird's-eye view from the 1890s lists many dozens of stores and services already serving a thriving community.

Besides the Steinway & Sons factory, the community thrived from the Steinway investments scattered throughout the hamlet, including the Astoria Mahogany Company, the Astoria Silk Works and the Steinway Transit Company. Everywhere was prosperity backed and supported by the Steinways.

Within twenty years, more than seven thousand people lived in the Steinway Settlement. William Steinway, in his diary, wrote, "Father would be proud."

Chapter 29

TEACH MY CHILDREN MUSIC

hy is music so important to us? Its purpose remains a mystery. It neither sustains the body nor propagates our species, yet it is innate within us, something every culture shares. It is so human to hum a tune, to tap to the beat. And for a very fortunate few who dedicate their lives to this art, we recall the words of Beethoven: "[They] force their way into it—for its secrets—to gain knowledge that can raise one to the divine."

Over two centuries, the Dulcken family—first as makers of musical instruments, then as performers on the stage and finally as teachers and managers of concert artists—brought music into the modern world. Starting with the courtly elite and then through the emerging middle class, they spread the beauty of instrument performance to a widening circle of patrons and pupils. They broke gender barriers as the first women to headline concerts with leading orchestras of their time. Their teaching methods, spanning the range from keyboard to string instruments, are taught to this day. And it is the good fortune that a son, Ferdinand Dulcken, was invited by another legend, William Steinway, to carry the muse of music to our city at a time—the mid-nineteenth century—when we were poised at the verge of greatness.

There was magic in this partnership between Steinway, a leading New York civic leader (who was also responsible for running the piano company), and Professor Dulcken, who managed Steinway Hall (and its stable of both Steinway artists and others, including the New York Philharmonic).

Furthermore, Dulcken's work in music education planted the seeds to sustain the growth of music arts beyond their lifetimes. During that feverish era, at the closing decades of the nineteenth century, Steinway Hall was the nation's stage, helping forge our city as the world capital of the arts and ideas.

It was also a time when these two men both called Astoria home. Thus, we have the testimony of Astorians who knew them personally. J.S. Kelsey's *History of Long Island City* (1896), the authoritative history of our community, was published by the *Long Island Star*, our newspaper of record. The book has extensive biographical sketches of both men. As to Professor Dulcken, it states (text is modernized from original):

Ferdinand Quentin Dulcken, from *History of Long Island City*, by J.S. Kelsey. *Public domain.*

> *No citizen of Long Island City has achieved more success in music. Professor Dulcken has the respect of those who know him as well as the general public. His ability as musical director, accompanist, pianist, and composer is universally recognized. He has earned a national reputation as the musical director for the greatest concert artists of our day, both here and abroad. From his headquarters in Steinway Hall, he has given instruction to those who are now famous in the musical world. Professor Dulcken has gained many triumphs in large festivals and critical recitals.*

Dulcken was an entrepreneur, promoter and artist manager who produced concerts, tours and other events in music. Legendary impresarios such as Thomas Beecham, Rudolf Bing, Sergei Diaghilev, Sol Hurok and those of today follow his pioneering footsteps. In addition, Dulcken developed modern practices in teaching music. Conservatories in New York such as the Juilliard School, Curtis Institute of Music, Manhattan School of Music, Mannes College and others still use the material and teaching principles established by Dulcken and his family.

Perhaps the most touching testimony to this man are entries in the diaries of his friend William Steinway. These legendary books (now at the Smithsonian) have scores of references painting a personal portrait of Ferdinand Dulcken. For example, here is a notation for a meeting with Steinway management discussing corporate strategy; there they are at the Steinway Mansion, sipping wine and playing cards with a circle of friends well into the night. The two even performed duets, with Dulcken at the keyboards and William singing, at impromptu gatherings and public events.

But perhaps the most telling of William's respect for the professor was this entry: "I have decided that Professor Dulcken will teach music to my children." One cannot find a better reference in music than that!

Despite protests, Dulcken's mansion and its recital hall, 31-07 31st Street, were torn down in 2018 after the Landmarks Preservation Commission stated it was unworthy of preservation.

Chapter 30

THE BLISSVILLE BANSHEE

*H*alloween is the time for recounting hauntings and scary stories. Long Island City has more than its share. Meet the Blissville Banshee.

The story started innocently enough in 1884 as James Flaherty, a wealthy florist of Blissville, was minding his business, wending his way home from Laurel Hill along a lane that headed toward Queens Boulevard. Passing some empty buildings at Calvary Cemetery, he was startled by a loud voice, high pitched as a woman's, moaning, "Oh ho!"

Thinking it was someone in distress, he rushed in and searched the house from "cellar to garret." He found nothing. While in the attic, he heard the wail again, but this time from outside the house. He looked out and saw nothing. At this point, more than just a "little frightened," he ran home.

On hearing the tale, his son John, described as a "strapping young man," immediately seized his shotgun and, forming a posse of ten friends, went on a wild pursuit of the "strange creature." Sure enough, they heard its cry, but now it seemed to be in the cemetery. They climbed the fence and searched among the tombstones. Around midnight, the voice faded and finally disappeared. Nothing was found.

The following day, word quickly spread throughout the suburban hamlets of Blissville, Laurel Hill and Long Island City Heights (which we now call Sunnyside). People came forward with confessions that they, too, had heard the sounds. Soon the word was out: all the locals would be "ready on Friday night" to "run down the Banshee." At nine o'clock that evening,

Eugène Delacroix French, Mephistopheles (1828). *Public domain.*

a bloodthirsty mob of one hundred vigilantes gathered in the barroom at Bradley's Hotel. Each one was armed with a six-shooter or shotgun.

With grim determination, they marched down the lane, approached and surrounded the same house where Flaherty had his frightening experience and stood whispering. The place had a reputation of being haunted. Rumor spread that several suicides had taken place in the immediate vicinity. Once again, the plaintive wail "Oh ho" was heard. After much considerable discussion, ten brave souls stormed into the house. Suddenly, a groan was distinctly heard from the cemetery. They rushed over the fence. Again, nothing was discovered. They returned home discouraged and disheartened but in agreement: the voice was not of any living creature.

Several aldermen, a local church sexton and even the assistant superintendent of Calvary Cemetery claimed to have heard the cry at night. Although most swore it was a ghost, or at least was not human, a local police officer who lived close to the cemetery claimed it was young men playing tricks on the community. A nearby judge thought it might be an owl.

An Irishman observed an old curse: "In the Owld Country whin the banshee com around, the handsomest girl in the neighborhood was sure to die. I don't mean to say that—God forbid it—but it doesn't look right ta me."

The locals maintained a watch but, fearing bad luck, soon started to refuse interviews with reporters. The story soon dropped from the public eye. But as neighbors continued to whisper among themselves on every tidbit of news, hysteria became entrenched, and a dark cloud descended along Newtown Creek. Women refused to walk the streets without their husbands. People did not venture out after dark. The local saloons and hotels, starved of business, began to close. People began to move away. Soon only a handful remained amid the grim detritus of nineteenth-century industry.

The banshee, undoubtedly grimly satisfied, remains at large.

Chapter 31

MAYOR "BATTLE AXE" GLEASON

Thank you to great-grandson Steven Morgan for information on Patrick Jerome "Battle Axe" Gleason, the last mayor of Long Island City.

Most of my knowledge of my great-grandfather Patrick Jerome "Battle Axe" Gleason comes from the various archives, my grandmother (his daughter) and other family members. But I will try!

First, Gleason was a politician and, although a businessman, too, not very good with finances. But despite his faults, he was always for the little guy—and for kids. But above all, he always tried to make Long Island City a better place, particularly for immigrants.

He was the Robert Moses of his time; he liked to build big-ticket items in infrastructure and education. Long Island City may not have been flush enough to pay for his projects, but that never mattered to him. He seemed to always think big. Indeed, he was not a detailed person concerned with today's costs or the future's needs.

Sadly, graft and corruption always come up in connection with his name. Jimmy Breslin once wrote that there are stories of Battle Axe throwing a bag of money over the side of a boat in the East River. I am guessing he wanted to improve the lives of families in the community. He was the driving force behind PS1, but then (as was the logic of that era), why not profit at the same time?

Much has been written about his greed, but we would like to believe he had a big heart and loved his daughter and the people of Long Island

City. He wanted to make life better for them during his tenure—at all cost!

Sure, he might have used his fists a bit too much when someone disagreed with him and perhaps, at times, lacked self-control when it came to access to power. But those were far different times than today, and I contend he helped put Long Island City on the map.

Having lost his wife (my great-grandmother) after she gave birth to his only child, Jessica (my grandmother), left a profound void in his life. As he was one of eight children in Ireland, I think that family and children were a priority in his life. For example, his affinity for the newspaper kids is legendary. I think he was less threatened by kids than by his adversaries.

Mayor Patrick Jerome Gleason, *New York Red Book* (1897). *Greater Astoria Historical Society.*

But then, I think he might have used relationships with children as a marketing tool for his business. Also, all of his moneymaking businesses (horsecar lines, real estate) would be enhanced if Long Island City was family friendly.

Interesting point: we always joked about our famous ancestor, his daughter, who seemed rich in Queens but not in upstate Cortland County. She had expensive taste, such as a Saks Fifth Avenue credit card, but no money; the bills were paid by her children when they arrived. I do remember some nice gifts years ago!

After my grandmother Jess passed away, I remember the trip down to Calvary Cemetery and listening to my uncles tell stories they heard from Jesse. Based on her accounts, Patrick Jerome Gleason was a saint. History may tell another story, but we will go with Grandma Jess's version.

I have a big package Mayor Bloomberg's office sent me after he did a speech at the Friendly Sons of St. Patrick dinner comparing himself to Mayor Gleason.

Thanks; this has been fun thinking and writing about "Battle Axe." Hope this helps.

Note: Thank you, indeed it does, sir! Gleason's life remains the great unwritten novel of New York City.

Chapter 32

HELL GATE GOLD

C aptain Kidd was rumored to have buried treasure in locations from the Caribbean to New England. After he was caught, his crew testified before the English Admiralty Courts and pointed out several places in the New York area where he had hidden caches of loot. In at least one location, the authorities uncovered treasure and rare cloths on Gardiner's Island, just outside Long Island's Great Peconic Bay.

Closer to Queens, generations of boys dug pits all over Maspeth in fruitless efforts at finding William Kidd's buried hoard. There was even a rumor that some of his crew lost cargo on the reefs beyond Hell Gate. Finally, in May 1897, a published newspaper account claimed that it might have been found.

On a spring day 115 years ago, Kate Woolsey of Woolsey Manor, Astoria (where the New York State Power Authority Power Plant now sits at Lawrence Point), retained some workers to work on her property. The location was called Casina Beach, a summer bathing location near North Beach Amusement Park.

The men had just turned over a large boulder. A small boy was seen around it, and after a bit, he left, carrying something in his hat. One of the men stopped him. The hat was full of "queer old coins." Most were silver; a few were gold. When questioned, the young lad said he had picked them up from the sand under the boulder's former location. He claimed ownership and refused to part with them. Woolsey was told about it. She sent for the boy and managed to secure some coins by giving him a silver dollar for each one.

Gold coins from the age of pirates. *Public domain.*

They ranged widely in date, with the earliest from the 1100s and the latest dated to the sixteenth century. Some were coined in England, one in Germany, another in Spain. Many had Arabic lettering (which would have made the 1100 dates correspond to the late 1600s in the western calendar). This was no surprise, as Kidd (and his contemporaries) commonly sailed into the Indian Ocean.

Most coins were too worn or corroded to make out much detail. One, however, was relatively well preserved. It was a fragile silver piece, reasonably round and about the size of a half dollar. It was identified as an Elizabethan shilling or crown and bore the date 1561. The inscription read: "Elizabeth, by the Grace of God, Queen of England, France, and Ireland."

The coin's date was just 140 years before Captain Kidd went to the scaffold in the execution dock in London. His death marked the end of the opening chapter in New York's history. The chaos of the colony's birth was now behind it. But for seventy-five years, it would remain a ward of England.

As to our mystery cache on the Astoria shore, the narrative relates nothing further. It should be no surprise, as shallow trenches with a few shovels of dirt hastily tossed over burlap bags in the dark of night would soon have their contents scattered along the shore by tide and storm. One could imagine gulls, attracted to the shiny "pebbles" on the waterfront, casually lining their nests with more wealth than most people would see at any one point in their lives.

It was somewhat ironic that, while many died in their pursuit to acquire wealth, most buried treasure ended up like this.

Chapter 33

THE CADENCE OF A SLEDGEHAMMER

*L*ong Island City has always been multinational, multicultural and multiracial. In the work gangs of its railroads, in the production lines of its factories and on the fields and pastures of its farms, your mettle—not the color of your skin—determined who you were.

From the sandhogs tunneling under the East River to the gandy dancers laying track on the Hell Gate, the ironworkers who walked the Queensboro beams and the human jackhammers hewing granite for its foundations, no one cared about your daddy. The gimlet eye of a supervisor only focused on a quota to fill, a tier of bricks to lay, a ship on Newtown Creek to unload. It was the cadence of the sledgehammer, not the color of one's skin, that tapped out the measure of a person's worth.

In colonial times, unlike in the South, a bondsman in New York had the right to seek new employment. But soon after independence, the state set slavery on the path to extinction. For decades before the Civil War, in what would later be Long Island City, a census taker could find no "slave" to enter on their charts. The rest of the country stood on the abyss of war, but the issue was already long decided by the Long Island City community. All people, of all colors and backgrounds, should get along and live together.

Diverse groups of faith congregations supporting one another transcended racial barriers. Great orators such as Booker T. Washington mounted its pulpits. A free community of Black people lived within the bounds of the township. From colonial times through emancipation, this location might have been a station on the Underground Railroad.

Flushing is justifiably proud of James Bland and Louis Latimer, but Long Island City had local legends such as "Back Number" Budd and the

A mason with a work gang shaping granite blocks for the Queensboro Bridge Queens Plaza, circa 1906, *New York City Archives.*

Brotherhood of Sleeping Car Porters. Its president, A. Philip Randolph, declared from the podium of the Civil Rights March on Washington in 1963: "Let the nation know the meaning of our numbers. We are not a pressure group. We are not an organization. We are not a mob. We are the advance guard of a massive moral revolution...not confined to the Negro, nor...confined to civil rights, for our white allies know that they are not free while we are not."

PART III
Gotham's Suburb
(1898–1960)

Chapter 34

WHOSE DOG ARE YOU?

New York in 1900 was a tough place for a mutt. A street waif was constantly dodging wagons and horses, tolerating children's taunts and the growls of filthy curs. Food was a scrap of meat from carrion found in the gutter. A glimmer of contentment could be gleaned from the gnawing of a bone that fell off a truck.

So it was no surprise that when a woman patted him on the head, he followed her onto a ferryboat and onto the warmth of a train car in Long Island City. He fell asleep under her seat. When he awoke, she was gone. Looking for his friend, he got off the car at the next stop. It was said that the stationmaster found him cowering and whimpering in the rain huddled next to a wall. Taking pity, he let him inside the station and fed him. The dog curled up and fell asleep. He was home.

The workers on the line adopted him and dubbed him Roxey (sometimes spelled Roxie or Roxy). They bought the pooch a nickel-plated collar inscribed, "I am Roxey, the LIRR dog. Whose dog are you?" Word of the new mascot reached the railroad's president, who issued a general order giving the dog rights over all passengers and employees on the system.

Although he now officially belonged to the board of directors, officials and employees, it was in the trainmen's private homes that he always found the latchstring out and a juicy bone awaiting him. While "working," Roxey's favorite place was perched on the locomotive fireman's seat, carefully keeping out of everyone's way, watching the scenery flash by outside his window.

"Roxie"
Long Island Railroad

Roxie, the Long Island Railroad mascot. *Public domain.*

One day, the porter assigned to President Theodore Roosevelt's private car found Roxey curled up, asleep on the bed. He tried to evict the dog. Upon hearing the commotion, the president walked in and inquired about the ruckus. He looked at the collar and backed off. The dog's privileges on the rail line outranked his.

Roxey's life pass on the Long Island Rail Road also extended to the Pennsylvania system (which had acquired the Long Island line). As with the typical commuter, he would leave Long Island City for Manhattan on a morning train and return later in the day (when he was ready) on a Queens-bound train. His favorite destination was the new Pennsylvania Station, which he frequently walked through on inspection tours.

Roxey had never been known to make an error when selecting trains. He always knew where he was going (at least if we accept the statements of his co-workers on the railroad). Therefore, it was a matter of wonder to all when he made a mistake one day in April 1911. He boarded a train for Pennsylvania Station, but instead of stopping in New York, he found himself on a through train that went straight to Philadelphia. Poor Roxey had to go, too. Probably no more indignant dog had ever landed at Philadelphia's Broad Street station.

The moment the train stopped and the doors opened, Roxey hopped out and ran down the platform, wheeled about a couple of times and let out a couple of yelps, which sounded suspiciously like canine swearing. He immediately selected a train headed back for New York and in five minutes was aboard at his usual post of duty.

He died in 1914. To this day, his monument is well tended by the employees of the Long Island Rail Road.

Chapter 35

THE PRIDE OF
A BEAUTIFUL WOMAN

S ettled by the Dutch in 1623, New York City is many islands linked both together and to the mainland by more than seventy-five bridges. Those major spans, constructed in the nineteenth and twentieth centuries, reflect the spirit of enthusiasm and determination of their age. Designed by creative engineering geniuses, these beautiful and imposing structures will stand for centuries.

Separating the boroughs at the heart of the city is the East River, a broad tidal channel. As the three cities on its banks—New York, Brooklyn and Long Island City—expanded and prospered, entrepreneurs, politicians and visionaries made plans to link them and bridge the dangerous waters. In time, it was spanned by the Brooklyn Bridge (1883), the Williamsburg Bridge (1903), the Queensboro Bridge (1909), the Manhattan Bridge (1909), Hell Gate Bridge (1917) and Triborough Bridge (1936). All are regarded as incredible feats of engineering

Following the success of the Brooklyn and Williamsburg Bridges, proposals for a third span to connect Midtown Manhattan and Long Island City, Queens, were met with enthusiasm by city leaders and the public. Earlier attempts to build a bridge at this location had failed. Most notable was the New York and Long Island Bridge Company, which went bankrupt in 1893.

It was to be designed by Gustav Lindenthal, commissioner of the new Department of Bridges, who envisioned it as a fusion of engineering and art design. Working with other engineers, he proposed a twin cantilever design with two spans connected by a smaller span over Roosevelt Island (then

Building the Queensboro Bridge looking north on Blackwells (Roosevelt Island), circa 1908. *New York City Archives.*

known as Blackwell's Island), a two-mile outcropping mid-channel between Manhattan and Queens.

Following many conflicts, including both design and personnel changes, the Queensboro Bridge was finally completed in late 1908. Finally, in March 1909, it was officially opened to the public with a grand ceremony at Queens Plaza, including a spectacular two-hour fireworks display.

The span had an immediate and profound effect on the development of Queens, changing it seemingly overnight from a largely rural area into a dense area of factories, transportation links and bedroom communities of model housing for the workers. Drowsy marshland became a hive whose labors fueled the coffers of a demanding New York City.

Architects describe the bridge as 7,449 feet long, with four 350-foot steel towers supported on stone piers and having interlacing steelwork adorned with small embellishments. Masonry approaches allow the passage of street traffic underneath. They are lined with attractive Guastavino tiles on the Manhattan side.

It is among the world's most heavily traveled bridges, carrying an average of 200,000 vehicles per day. Each year, it's featured on international television when it is closed to traffic for the running of the New York Marathon.

With its graceful symmetry, this massive steel giant continues to be a source of inspiration for artists, songwriters and authors. *Spider-Man* would not have been the same without this particular bridge. Until their first visit to New York, many knew it only as the 59th Street Bridge because of the Art Garfunkel song. Families with roots in Manhattan call it the 59th Street Bridge; those with a Queens background refer to it as the Queensboro Bridge.

Lin Yutang, in *Chinatown Family*, wrote, "The bridge had the sweep of the sea…the grace and strength of a great work of art, and the independence and pride of a beautiful woman."

Chapter 36

A BRIDGE WITHOUT EQUAL

*T*he Hell Gate Bridge opened to passenger rail revenue service on April 1, 1917, creating a continuous all-rail link between Boston and Washington, D.C., via New York City. The bridge, spanning the East River at the Hell Gate, is the centerpiece of a complex network of bridges and viaducts that links Astoria, Queens, on Long Island with the mainland in the Bronx via Ward's and Randall's Islands. It was the last major link in the national rail network connecting rail traffic on Long Island directly to the rest of the nation. It is a lynchpin of the Northeast Corridor (Washington, D.C.–New York City–Boston), considered the most critical section of the national rail network.

Since the mid-nineteenth century, the dream of a rail bridge to Long Island had been on the books. Still, the challenging topography of New York Harbor and the restrictions placed on East River bridges by the Brooklyn Navy Yard made one proposal after another impractical. Finally, in the latter part of the nineteenth century, a syndicate involving the Steinways tried to raise money for a regional rail network. Still, it fell victim to the recurring financial panics during that era.

The Steinways decided to move forward with a much smaller trolley tunnel between Long Island and Manhattan, but that was halted by an accidental fatal dynamite explosion (see chapter 38).

Enter the Pennsylvania Railroad, which at the time had 250,000 employees and an annual budget greater than the federal government. The railroad

The dedication ceremony of the Hell Gate Bridge. Chief designer Gustav Lindenthal turns the bridge over to J.A. McCrea, president of the New York Connecting Railroad, March 10, 1917. *Amtrak.*

had the resources to privately fund the bridge and its feeder lines. It is 8.96 miles long and cost $27 million to construct (more than a half billion dollars in today's money).

Something on this scale for a railroad bridge had never been attempted before—nor has it been equaled. It remains the longest and heaviest steel bridge in the world. Yet many believe it is the ultimate bridge in both utility and beauty.

Hell Gate Bridge engineer Gustav Lindenthal, who was also involved in the Queensboro Bridge, assembled a team that would be designing bridges for a generation: architect Henry Hornbostel, who collaborated on the Queensboro Bridge, and assistant Othmar Ammann, who carried the legacy forward with bridge design through the 1960s by designing the George Washington, Throgs Neck and Verrazano Narrows bridges

It was quite a challenge on many levels. The Hell Gate Strait, which connects Long Island Sound with the East River, here measured as deep as two hundred feet in places, the deepest part of New York Harbor. The Randall's Island pier is anchored by a bridge that straddles both sides of an inactive fault deep underground.

When the two sides met, they were less than an inch off, giving us some idea of the precise calculations that went into the bridge construction in an era of paper and pencil decades before mathematical calculations were crunched out on a computer.

The first revenue passenger train to use the Hell Gate Bridge was the Federal Express, which traveled overnight between Boston and Washington, D.C. Currently, approximately forty daily passenger trains cross the bridge each day, as well as freight trains.

For a century, outside of a few coats of paint, the Hell Gate has needed no major repairs. Pundits believe that should civilization disappear, the bridge would last thousands of years and would be one of the last vestiges of New York City to be reclaimed by nature.

Chapter 37

GRAPE LEAVES IN THE LOBBY

Thank you to nephew Milton Mathews and other members of the Mathews family for information on Gustave X. Mathews.

*I*t was September 1916, the midpoint of World War I. The blood of one thousand years of European culture and history flowed into the mud of Flanders Fields and the Russian steppes. The future's promise was but a faint glimmer on a horizon obscured by dust and smoke of a holocaust that was to last, with fits and starts, for a generation.

But in America, New York City's largest borough, Queens, was already looking to the future. Less than two decades after becoming part of Greater New York and a decade after opening a direct link to Manhattan via the Queensboro Bridge, the city's transportation network reached deep into the borough. By 1916, the Ditmars elevated train had opened (which was then planned to continue to North Beach, today's LaGuardia Airport), as had the Corona elevated train (before it reached Flushing). The borough was now open and ready for business.

In 1916, the G.X. Mathews Company submitted one-quarter of all building permits in the borough—a feat never again equaled. By September of that year, news outlets announced that the Mathews Building Company had acquired a vast expanse of undeveloped land east of Steinway Street. Hundreds of the still ubiquitous Mathews Model Flats would soon sprout from more than five hundred empty lots.

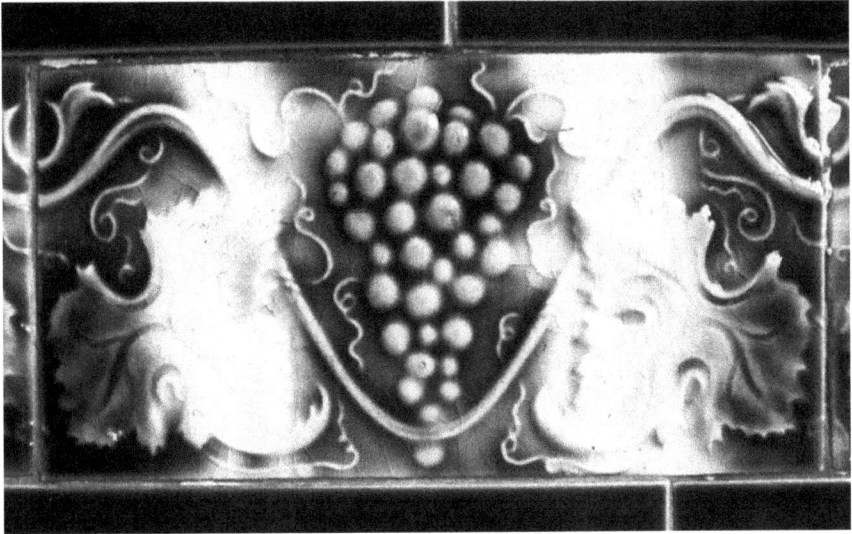

Tiles in the vestibule of a Matthews Model Flat. *Greater Astoria Historical Society*

For the next decade, along 30th and 34th Avenues, down 48th and 43rd Streets and over to Sunnyside and Woodside, Queens, the city witnessed the most successful building venture tailored to meet the needs of the traditionally neglected market for housing: homes for working people. They were called Mathews Model Flats.

Company president Ernest Mathews proudly proclaimed, "The fact is more evident day by day that Long Island City and its adjacent sections are logical residential sections...for those dissatisfied with conditions in the over-crowded sections of Manhattan and Brooklyn.... The advantage is ours because of our close proximity to the heart of the greatest city in the world."

The firm was started by an older brother, Gustave Xavier Mathews, a Bavarian who, after making that momentous decision to immigrate to America, faced his new future behind a pushcart hawking flowers. Gustave's good fortune was to marry the daughter of a builder (as family legend tells us). So he decided to follow his father-in-law's vocation. His life, and our city, profited enormously from that union.

G.X. had a simple business model: build with principle; apply only the finest possible materials (he used non-combustible Kreischerville Brick), design attractive façades (he used prominent architect Louis Allmendinger), insist on healthy apartment layouts (a window in every room) and fix an affordable price tag (hundreds of buildings were sold without a single foreclosure). It seems G.X. was a Socialist. He built only for the working class. Years later, when Metropolitan Life Insurance, which financed his purchasers' mortgages, asked him to build Stuyvesant Town, he refused. Its targeted market was too middle class for his tastes.

When the First World War broke out in Europe, Gustave had a small fortune locked up in Germany. Although the United States was still neutral, currency controls forbade him to take money out of Germany. Undeterred, he converted his cash to wine, exported it to neutral Switzerland, sold it and brought his wealth to the United States.

He used that money to build a block of buildings on both sides of 48th Street between Broadway and 34th Avenue. Metal rationing during World War I may have stopped him from placing metal cornices on every building on the block, but he made sure to have terra-cotta grape motifs in every lobby—a legacy of a clever man.

Chapter 38

STEINWAY RAPID TRANSIT

*A*fter conquering the world of music and ascending the pinnacle of New York's cultural scene with America's premier entertainment and lecture space, Steinway Hall, the Steinway family turned their interests toward the "high tech" of their age: transportation.

The family needed to ensure that workers and residents in their community could have the best of both worlds: easy access to big-city Manhattan and the advantages of living in a small town like the Steinway community in Long Island City. Besides, there were all those empty lots in their settlement that had to be sold. So again, transportation easy and cheap was the key.

Their deep pockets made the chronically ailing Long Island City streetcar lines easy prey. However, the family's legendary brilliance at problem-solving ensured that those street rails not only ran on time but were also soon expanded into a regional network. In 1883, William Steinway incorporated the Steinway & Hunter's Point Railroad Company as a holding company after merging the Long Island City street railways into one entity. He built a massive car depot with shops, offices and storage areas on the west side of Steinway Street above 20th Avenue.

The Steinways were just getting started.

During an 1888 trip to Europe, William met Gottlieb Daimler, who held patents on gasoline's first practical internal combustion engine. After the two took a ten-mile drive in Daimler's new horseless carriage, Steinway and Daimler agreed to a partnership, Daimler Motor Company, which would initially focus its attention on stand-alone engines and motorboat production.

Steinway president Frederick Steinway receiving the controller from the motorman at the end of the first train ride to Ditmars Station. Queens Borough president Maurice Connelly is looking on. February 1, 1917. *Henry Steinway Collection, Greater Astoria Historical Society.*

Although American roads, unlike those in Europe, were not yet ready for automobiles, towns and cities around the country were in the midst of a great boom in street and highway construction. Thus, it was only a matter of time before the American public would be receptive to the automobile.

Their first shop was a little building on the east side of Steinway Street between 20th Avenue and 20th Road in 1890. One could argue the Automotive Age truly began there, for at this time, Henry Ford, still feeding teaspoons of gasoline to an experimental motor in his wife's kitchen, had not yet built a workable engine.

In the early 1890s, William, as chair of the New York City subway commission, helped design the city's transit network. On paper, a series of lines was drawn connecting the Bronx and Brooklyn with Manhattan. However, within Queens, only the Long Island City/Astoria areas, already served by his transit interests, were scheduled to be fully integrated within the embryonic subway network. His dream remains incomplete to this day: the 31st Street elevated line stops at Ditmars Boulevard. Then, it was to reach North Beach, today's LaGuardia Airport.

In 1892, the Steinway Railway company undertook a large-scale engineering project after William Steinway decided to switch from horsepower to electrification of the street railway network. He built a great power plant to furnish power for his piano factory and the local community.

Things suddenly took a quick turn. Daimler, beset by legal problems, could not contribute his share of the joint venture. Patience wore thin. "I have serious apprehensions as to monetary outlook," William wrote in his diary, "and curse it's draining me of money and resolve to stop it."

William's troubles were just beginning, as his health was failing. A planned East River Tunnel linking the intersection of Vernon and Jackson with the Grand Central Terminal was halted after only a few months when a tremendous explosion killed and injured scores of people.

In a scramble to retrench, the Steinways sold their traction interests to a Philadelphia syndicate in the fall of 1895. The new entity, the New York and Queens Railway, completed his dream to knit the scattered hamlets and villages of Queens together.

When William Steinway died in 1896, the Steinways liquidated their Daimler interests (the factory had built only one automobile). Instead, they relinquished a role in transportation projects such as the Queensboro Bridge and the East River Tunnel. Nephews studying transportation engineering were called back to the factory to run departments that made pianos. The Daimler factory, entangled in legal suits and restrictive tariffs, was destroyed in a 1907 fire.

The late Henry Z. Steinway, who had an office in Steinway Hall, had a fascinating collection of Steinway memorabilia. One of the items was a map attached to a prospectus that outlined plans for a vast New York metropolitan transit system. A single rail line linked New Jersey with Manhattan, Long Island and New England. Tunnels were planned under the Hudson and East Rivers. A viaduct headed up 21st Street and crossed into the Bronx through a bridge over the Hell Gate. It was dated sometime in the 1880s.

Throughout the closing decades of the nineteenth century, the country remained locked in a depression. The Steinways never could raise money for their dream. It remained in a file cabinet, forgotten, for a century. Later, the plans were shown to historians.

William's New York subway network collected its first fare in 1904. The East River tunnel still called the "Steinway Tubes" opened in 1915 (the 7 train runs through it). By 1918, automobiles were commonplace.

If William could have lived a few years into the twentieth century, the final chapter would have been very different. Then, corporate trusts and monopolies could command sums of money undreamed of by families as wealthy as the Steinways. By 1917, the Pennsylvania Railroad had brushed off those forty-year-old plans found in Henry's cabinet. Instead, that railroad went on to build the Sunnyside Yards, Pennsylvania Station and a rail system that connected our city to New England and the American heartland.

One can argue that Long Island City, the borough of Queens, the city of New York and our metropolitan region developed in the ways they did because of those dreams the Steinways had while looking out over their village from a mansion on an Astoria hill.

If only William had reached his mid-eighties, he would have seen his dreams become a reality.

Chapter 39

THE LAST LICENSE

*I*t would go down as one of the most brutal winters of New York's history, with record snowfall. A few minutes before midnight on January 17, 1920, the temperature fell toward the single digits. The snow that had been on the ground for a few days had turned into a sheet of ice.

That evening, no one wanted to go home. In Manhattan, flappers were dancing with their tuxedoed swells at Midtown nightspots. In Minden House, a legendary taproom in Jamaica, Queens, a group of serious men, one in priestly garb, sat with a small casket over a ritual dubbed the "funeral of John Barleycorn." That evening, the taps in bars and saloons around the country were to be turned off. Permanently.

Some called it the Noble Experiment; for others, at midnight, it would be the final "last call." A new law, Prohibition, was about to ban the production, transportation and sale of alcoholic beverages.

Although its advocates talked about the evils of liquor, the law's purpose was to target immigrant populations residing in large urban areas in eastern cities. Two-thirds of all states, primarily rural and in the South and West, were already dry. The law was passed aimed explicitly at those ethnic enclaves.

We can imagine what it was like at Bohemian Hall in Astoria at the Bohemian Citizens' Benevolent Society with working men, bearing such typical Czech names as Emil, Rudolf, Pavel and Josef, standing, cradling their beers, heads bowed in sober conversation. Prohibition was a dagger to the very heart of their culture. Yet in the minutes leading up to midnight, no one was leaving.

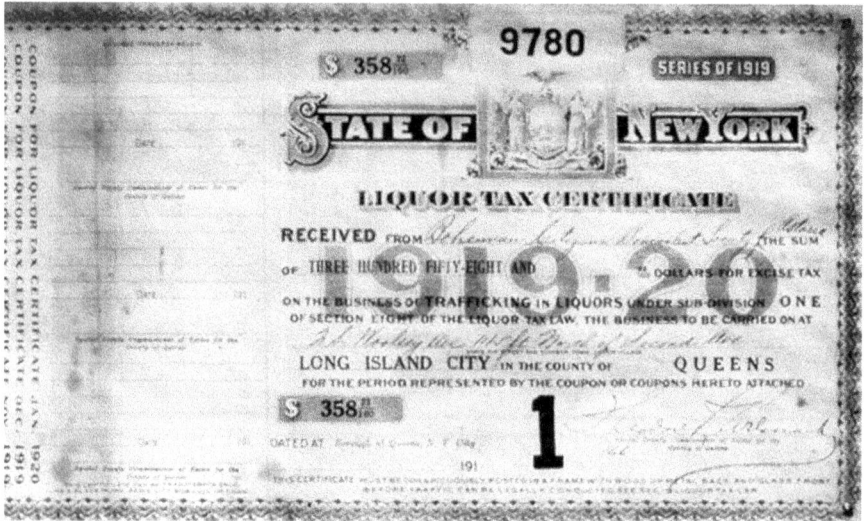

New York City liquor license, 1919–20, Bohemian Citizens' Benevolent Society. *Greater Astoria Historical Society.*

The cornerstone of the building for the Bohemian Hall was laid in 1910. Stubborn and steadfast to their values in the face of the oncoming dry tide, they went ahead in 1919 and purchased for their park one of the last liquor licenses issued by New York City. Czechs have the world's highest beer consumption. Beer was literally cheaper than water. The traditions of craft brewing went back one thousand years; hop cultivation went back two thousand. Beer gardens were at the heart of their culture as places for the community to gather on weekends. In the beer garden, men talked of politics and work; women kept a keen eye on their children and exchanged news.

Around the country, the clock chimed that last moment at midnight. An eyewitness later wrote, "Lights were switched off and on to announce the hour. Some who were drinking from glasses carried them away. Others who had bottles in their hands about to pour drinks carried them off. No one stopped them." We cannot imagine the sad journey home from Bohemian Hall that night, but we have a good sense of their resolve in continuing their traditions. The liquor license stayed on the wall.

The Czech community sustained Bohemian Hall through Prohibition, the Depression, World War II and changing demographics. In the 1990s, when they threw open the doors to the public, a new generation discovered its beauty, spawning a new national awareness of beer gardens and craft beer. It is the last authentic old-time beer garden in New York. The 1919–20 liquor license is still on display.

Chapter 40

A HIP-POCKET BLOW-OUT

*I*t was the winter of 1921. Prohibition, the ban on alcoholic beverages passed by Congress a year before, shakily started its second year. For the annual dinner of the Police Lieutenants Benevolent Association at the Hotel Commodore, the rank and file spread the word that it was to be the "liveliest time in years." Among the 1,600 police lieutenants and their guests, the name of Mr. Volstead, the congressman responsible for Prohibition, was not on the seating list and not in evidence on the dais.

Probably half of those who entered the dining room, both in uniform and full dress, carried mysterious suitcases, handbags and wrapped bundles. The event was already in serious trouble when a large contingent of police from Queens and their friends arrived; many were from Long Island City (the accounts stated firmly). Several of those who came empty-handed were the recipients of small bottles containing a dark fluid that was liberally passed around the ballroom. The demand was so great that the supply soon ran out. The "fluid" later was poured into glass pitchers of lemonade placed on the tables. It apparently added to the tastiness of the drink, for the waiters were kept busy filling pitchers all evening. There was general agreement that the "lemonade" had plenty of pep.

The program was to start during a ten-minute recess before dinner. After fifteen minutes, members of the Dinner Committee, walking up and down aisles, failed to restore order. Guests, with "capacious and hospitable hip pockets filled with cheerfulness greater than any half-percent alcohol could ever produce," were so noisy that speakers could not be heard even with the pleading of strong-lunged lieutenants. The event began to fall apart.

Men drinking, circa 1920s. *Public domain.*

Rear Admiral James Glennon, commander of the Naval District, tried to shout over the din. Reporters at the end of the speakers' table could barely hear him. Finally, he sat down, grousing, "Why can't they shut up down there?" General George Wingate stood to speak and then sat down. The bedlam bumped up a few notches every time a distinguished guest moved toward the podium

Mayor Hylan was introduced. Taking a different tack, he started by threatening, "The police commissioner demands silence, or he will call in the police!" There was an outburst of applause. Then, echoing an old political campaign chant, the spectators on the left side of the room cried out, "What's the matter with Hylan?" Revelers on the right side enjoined, "Oh, he's all right!"

Tossing his speech aside, the mayor praised the department and wound up calling Police Commissioner Enright "the NYPD's greatest commissioner" amid shouts of praise. Governor Edward Edwards of New Jersey, the next speaker, evoked more cheers by stating, "New Jersey is the wettest state in the Union." He raised an empty glass to his lips and smiled, which prompted an ovation.

Governor Al Smith; Father Francis Duffy, chaplain of the Fighting 69th; and Police Commissioner Enright followed in rapid succession. As he was leaving, Smith got a laugh when he said, "Lord knows, but we did what we could to kill that lemonade off!"

The Police Lieutenants' Ball was over, and although it took another decade for Congress to finally accept it, it was also the night that Prohibition died.

Chapter 41

A FORD CAR
WITH A BREWSTER BODY

Thank you to the late Alan Baum, whose father was a key employee of the Brewster Automobile Company.

ames Brewster, a direct descendant of Elder William Brewster of the Plymouth Colony, founded the Brewster Carriage Company. He was born in 1788, and while he could have gone to the college of his choice, he was a disciple of Benjamin Franklin and chose to apprentice himself to a carriage maker in Northampton, Massachusetts, at age fifteen. In 1809, while traveling by coach to New York, the coach broke down in New Haven. While waiting for repairs, he visited a local coach maker, John Cook, and decided to work for him. A year later, he opened his own business. He was very successful and opened branches in Bridgeport and New York City. He had two sons, James and Henry, who took over the company when he retired in 1856.

Henry enjoyed the good life and moved the headquarters to New York City. Henry had a son, William Brewster "W.B.," who, like his grandfather, refused college and apprenticed himself to the company at five dollars a week in 1883. He soon took over the company, which apparently delighted his father. In 1898, Alan Baum's father, Seymour Baum, a twelve-year-old youngster, joined the firm as an office boy. At that time, the firm was in the Times Square area.

The firm had been enormously successful. One of the stories told is that someone once remarked that Brewster's was the Tiffany of the carriage

The 1932 Plymouth Brewster Town Car, customized by Brewster & Co. for the family of President Franklin Delano Roosevelt. Automobile Driving Museum, El Segundo, California. *Daderot, public domain.*

companies. The other person is said to have replied that quite the contrary, "Tiffany is the Brewster's of the jewelry business."

Alan Baum said that for some reason, W.B. took his father under his wing and trained him. Brewster's had slowly shifted from carriages to automobiles in the early twentieth century. At that time, many automobile companies made the chassis and hired someone else to do the body. So, for example, almost all of the American Rolls-Royce chassis had the bodies put on by Brewster's. They did the same thing for other automobiles, including a French manufacturer and even an occasional Ford, in addition to their car, the Brewster.

In 1910, William moved the headquarters and facilities to Long Island City and built the Brewster building on Queens Plaza. During World War I, Brewster became involved in aviation. Its main product was wooden propellers, and many portions of the early planes were also made of wood. In the meantime, Alan's father was steadily rising in importance in the firm. W.B. encouraged him to spend some time with other firms to see their methods of manufacture

In the mid-'20s, Brewster became more involved in aviation, and Alan's father headed that division. Around that time, GM considered purchasing the company, but that never materialized. By 1927, Mr. Baum was managing the firm for W.B. In 1929, he decided to establish his own business, and W.B. not only encouraged him but also invested in it. The plant was adjacent to the Long Island Rail Road at the Elmhurst-Woodside border. It later became the General Diaper plant. However, by 1932, with the Depression, both the General Diaper plant and the Brewster business were in trouble. By the mid-'30s, W.B. had decided to close. Alan Baum's father, who had moved his company back to the Brewster, handled the closure and managed the building for the family.

There were several cars left over or not claimed that Alan's father had to dispose of as well. One of them was sold to Lou Reisner, who managed Fairchild Aviation in Hagerstown, Maryland. The car, a Rolls-Royce convertible, was sold to him for fifty dollars. A man named John Inskip spent several months restoring the car, and when he finished, it was a thing of beauty.

One of the tenants was Brewster Aircraft, which had absolutely nothing to do with the Brewster family, and the family was very unhappy with the use of their name. The head of that firm was a Mr. Work, a former naval inspector. That firm left the building during World War II and merged with Republic Aviation in Farmingdale.

Another tenant was Diorama Corporation, which in the late '30s made a diorama of New York City with every building as it was, even if they were under construction. That was done for the World's Fair of 1939. It was fascinating to see the changes they would make weekly.

Alan's father was responsible for distributing the records and documents to varied museums. They were fascinating. He remembers one promissory note signed by A. Lincoln for a carriage he was purchasing with time payments. There was great old Americana, things like the first license plate issued by the State of New Jersey and priceless old coaching horns. Some of these items went to the Ford Museum because in 1937 or 1938, Henry Ford came to the Baum house in Flushing to thank Alan's father, whom he knew, for sending them to him. Henry Ford stayed the day and had dinner with the family.

Chapter 42

THE STORY OF
MICHAEL CASALINO

*I*t is 1921. A young man is about to die. He is the first person from Queens to be executed in twenty-three years. The grim story of Astoria's Michael Casalino unfolds. Welcome to death row in Sing Sing Prison (today the Sing Sing Correctional Facility in Ossining, New York).

Convicted in the old Long Island City Courthouse for the deaths of former Astorians Mr. and Mrs. Joseph Holbach, the young man is about to meet his doom. He is calm and composed, without flinching or bravado; even veteran guards rate him as one of the "gamest men to sit in the chair."

It need not have turned out like this. Casalino, one of six men who held up Joseph and Helen Holbach in their bar, turned over evidence against "Little Joe" Zambelli, the gang's ringleader. Casalino thought his sentence would be commuted to life. Although Zambelli was duly convicted for his part in the murder and was sentenced to death because of the testimony, New York governor Nathan Miller refused to commute Casalino's sentence.

It is now his last day on earth. He is given his last meal. For dessert, Casalino requests a strawberry shortcake, which arrives from the warden's kitchen. With just five hours before his execution, his heartbroken young wife makes her visit bearing more devastating news: for the first time, he learns that both of his children had died during his two-year confinement in the death house. They were victims of the great flu pandemic of 1919. His wife had kept the news from him until her hope for her husband disappeared. Finally, she shows him a photo of the youngest child. Its tiny body lay in a coffin.

After she leaves, he spends his last hours with a priest.

Warden, guards and a cellblock in Sing Sing-Prison. *George Bain Collection, Library of Congress, Prints and Photographs Division.*

It is now time. As the inmate begins that last walk to the execution chamber, Casalino calls out to Zambelli, "Goodbye. I wish you luck. I hope you get a new trial." Zambelli's response is lost by a chorus of farewells from the other twenty-two occupants of the death house. Finally, one calls out, "We know you are innocent, Mike."

In another part of town, the final players of the drama assemble. Sixteen men reported by "invitation" are preparing to attend the execution. Ossining is gloomy to the eye and spirit as they make their way from the New York train to the prison. The prison entrance is reached by a winding wooden stairway snaking up the hill. At the top, lights twinkle as the buildings are bathed in light. They hear whistling and even a snatch of a song through steel-barred windows.

They meet at the somber gates of Sing Sing, but no one takes notice. This is the prison's eighth execution in five months. Inside the entrance, they are told to make themselves at home while Principal Keeper McIntyre examines their credentials.

A small man oddly dressed in rough but neat clothing sits quietly in the corner. His black shoes shine immaculately. The guards know him, and the witnesses learn that he is John Hurlburt, state electrician. He is the person who sends prisoners to their deaths in the electric chair for $150 a head.

The sixteen witnesses for the execution are invited into the warden's office. They stand in a semicircle. Their credentials are again examined. Joining them is Dr. Amos Squires, the prison physician, and his assistant. The state electrician disappears.

The witnesses are an odd assemblage. They include two dentists from Jamaica, a chauffeur, a naval lieutenant, two shopkeepers from Ossining, a Paris reporter traveling around the world studying methods of capital punishment and representatives of the Queens County sheriff and the Queens district attorney's office.

As the reporter from the Paris newspaper makes notes, the lieutenant draws off by himself and talks to no one. The dentists find company enough by themselves. The chauffeur, who drove from Briarcliffe, parked his employer's car outside. He expresses hope that his two kids inside are asleep.

Major Lewis Lawes, the warden of Sing Sing, addresses the men: "Gentlemen, you know why you are here. When you pass the death house, please observe silence." He takes out his watch. They stand silently; nobody so much as whispers. Outside his office, the switchboard suddenly buzzes. The warden looks up anxiously. Quickly, the receptionist answers it. The call is not from Albany. There will be no reprieve.

At one minute before midnight, Warden Lawes signals to start. He instructs the witnesses to form a column and marches them out two by two. The warden is at the head. The witnesses stumble in the darkness before reaching a heavy steel gate between two stone piers. "Open up!" orders Warden Lawes to a rifle-bearing sentry dimly silhouetted against the sky. The gate slides noiselessly up, and the party enters.

A small yellow building stands out in the darkness. It looks like a chapel, but it is the death house. A door opens, and a brilliant shaft of light falls through. As they enter, a keeper orders, "Gentlemen, remove your hats." The room is aglow, with light reflected off the buff-colored ceiling and walls. It could be a hospital ward. But unlike the movies, there is nothing dark or drab. They sit on four pew-like benches.

The sinister thing stands in the center of the room, bathed in a powerful light. It is not a heavy, clumsy-looking chair, as imagined, but a lightly constructed chair made of oak. On either side are three guards. Dr. Squires and his assistant stand in front of the chair. The electrician is by the switchboard fussing with a little switch.

All eyes are on the door. Then, audible to those in the witness seats, comes the tread of feet in slow cadence. Finally, there is the low rumble of voices in prayer and the answer of another voice. In comes Principal Keeper McIntyre, with a portly priest, followed by a bareheaded and disheveled-looking young man in loose-fitting, flapping trousers. He wears a white shirt with the neck cut away. He does not shrink or hesitate. In his hands, he carries a black crucifix. He listens for a moment as the priest recites the Litany of the Saints. "Ora Pro Nobis," Mike answers. His stockinged feet make no sound on the floor.

He sits down. His arms are strapped in, and the electrode is attached to his head. Before the black hood is placed over his face, the condemned man blurts out, "Dr. Squires, shake my hand. You have always been kind to me. Goodbye to all of you. I thank you for what you have done for me."

Dr. Squires grasps his hand, steps back and then gives a signal to the man at the switchboard. A switch snaps.

Mike Casalino was twenty-four years old.

Chapter 43

I OWE IT TO YOU

arcus Loew was born to a poor Jewish family in New York City. Forced to leave school at a young age and work at a series of menial jobs, he was fortunate to land a job on a ferryboat and was able to save a nest egg to invest in a penny arcade business. Soon he was buying nickelodeons and began to build a chain of theaters.

It was one thing having venues to show entertainment; filling them with quality programs was the next step. So Loew began to acquire a stable of vaudeville acts, variety shows and one-reeler films. He purchased several chains, including Metro Pictures and Goldwyn Picture Corporation (including its "Leo the Lion" trademark). He was an integral part of that legendary first generation responsible for starting the motion picture industry, including Lee Shubert, Samuel Goldwyn, Nicholas Schenck, Louis B. Mayer and Irving Thalberg.

In the early 1920s, however, the industry was still going through its growing pains. It was slowly gravitating to California, a place Loew was loath to relocate to, and his sprawling portfolio of theaters and entertainment content lacked a cohesive command structure. Wise in acknowledging his limitations, he hired an extraordinary team to run his conglomerate and mentored a generation of theater managers and production executives.

Loew's Theatres became the most prestigious chain of movie theaters in the United States. MGM Motion Pictures' financing arm soon passed Universal Pictures as the most prominent global motion picture firm.

In Astoria, a protégé of Loew's, Michael Glynne, opened the Astoria Theater on November 22, 1920, at the corner of 30th Avenue and Steinway Street, a location that ensured it would be an instant success. Shapiro and Sons were the architects for the 2,800-seat venue.

The opening night bill offered "high-class vaudeville and the finest feature photo-plays." Music was provided by both a symphony orchestra and a $25,000 concert organ. Evening shows, which ran from 7:00 p.m. to 11:00 p.m., alternated between live performances and movies. Seats ranged from twenty to seventy-five cents and could be reserved for the entire season.

It was an instant success.

Portrait of Marcus Loew. From *The Businessman in the Amusement World*, by Robert Grau. *Public domain.*

In January 1923, three years after it opened, the chain of theaters managed by Glynne and his partner Ward, including the Astoria, was sold to Loew as a friendly merger. Glynne remained in residence, and at the inaugural program under the new management, Marcus Loew, the featured speaker, heaped praise on his former assistant.

The evening was described as an unforgettable event for those who could crowd into the theater that evening. Four hours of live vaudeville and a short movie went on until midnight. In a show of support for Mr. Loew, dozens of motion picture stars were in the audience. The audience roared with delight at the antics of comedians as they sold popcorn and peanuts in the aisles. After the entertainers sorted themselves out, Queens borough president Maurice Connelly, who led a delegation of officials, briefly stood up to heap praise on everyone present. But the true moment of the evening came when Marcus Loew himself took the stage and revealed something about his past that made the occasion truly special.

"I feel that I owe it to you," he started as those present quieted to a hush, "to tell you what is on my mind. I wish I could tell you how deeply I feel at this moment." He paused. "I have always wanted to come back to Astoria. You see, when I was a boy, I sold candy on the Astoria Ferry. All the people seemed to have plenty of money, and many were generous. At that time, it was the most profitable source of money for me and helped me get started."

He brought down the house.

Loew never got to see the dynamo that MGM was to become. He died three years later of a heart attack at the age of fifty-seven in Glen Cove, New York, and according to Wikipedia, he was interred in the Maimonides Cemetery in Brooklyn. For his significant contribution to the motion picture industry's development, Marcus Loew has a star on the Hollywood Walk of Fame at 1617 Vine Street. To this day, the Loew name is synonymous with movie theaters.

Chapter 44

ADMIRAL OF THE CITY FLEET

C aptain Will Hamilton, of 41–23 76th Street, Elmhurst, known in the harbor as "Admiral of the City Fleet," got his start on the 34th Street run. When he was interviewed in 1925 while captain of the *Macon* on the Staten Island Ferry, he claimed that he still missed his East River run. "I left with regret, for I spent the better part of my life on that boat."

Crowds that went to the race track and the German picnic parties heralded the opening of "Beer Season." I used to carry about 40,000 racetrack followers in a day, about 10,000 in one hour—in addition to the regular crowd! That group was good-natured and orderly. Every prizefighter was above board, and I knew them all by sight. They were herded on like cattle, but there was never rowdiness.

Everyone who became captain had to work his way from deckhand. I became a deckhand when the auto came into vogue. There was a law that cars could not go on or off on their own power. So most of the cars were pushed off the boat by deckhands who made a little extra change. One day a wealthy man gave me all the change in his pocket. I counted it later. It was $2.60 in coins! Another source of revenue for deckhands was stowing coaches on the ferry boats. We used to get all the funeral processions that went to Calvary Cemetery. We could make room for an extra coach by watching the deck closely after the boat was loaded. I used to collect fifty cents for that effort.

Long Island City Ferry Terminal. *Greater Astoria Historical Society.*

Near its two terminals were popular watering holes, Tony Miller's in Long Island City, and McSherry's on the Manhattan side. Many male passengers stopped at these places, and some could not walk onboard in a straight line. At Miller's Place, a bell would ring in the barroom warning the men that the boat was about to leave. A wild scramble followed. Sometimes the bell rang a little prematurely, and the imbibers filed back into the saloon again and ordered another round.

The 34th Street Ferry was responsible for giving Mayor Gleason of Long Island City his nom de guerre, "Battle Axe" that he used in his campaign for elections. "Paddy" Gleason deducted that the railroad people discriminated against outside teamsters by allowing express wagons to take possession of the front of the line enabling them to get on the boats first. The railroad set up poles in front of the ferry to keep the express wagons in line. The poles blocked the outside wagons from getting aboard. One morning, Gleason came to the ferry with a force of men with axes and cut the poles down. I saw this myself. There was also a goodly number in a crowd of spectators who were quite delighted with the proceedings and cheered Gleason on.

He was a clever politician, uneducated—but in his own way, got the votes. Cutting down those poles was one of his ways of keeping himself before the public as the defender of the people's rights. His valet, a fellow named "Scotty," either in remorse of Gleason's death or from too much liquor, jumped off the boat one night. Reginald Brooks of the Meadowbrook Hunt Club, a millionaire, jumped overboard to save him. He got a Congressional medal, I recall.

I used to have a nodding acquaintance with every millionaire that comes to Long Island, including the Belmonts, Whitneys, and the Mackays. There used to be six boats to 34ʰ Street, two to James Slip, and three fast steamers that were special and conveyed the bankers to Wall Street. The bankers did not want to mix with the common herd that traveled to James Slip. Those 20 mph boats were practically yachts. They were scheduled to arrive at the terminal to meet trains that came from the millionaire colony.

Chapter 45

THE LAST FERRY

*T*he Long Island Rail Road has made an announcement: on March 5, 1925, the Hunter's Point Ferry will pass into history. Until the very end, the city had vowed to fight to keep the service. Still, everyone knew that the Long Island City transportation institution, antedating the Civil War, would go out of existence.

The announcement read that the last boats were scheduled to leave their terminals at precisely 6:48 p.m. The fifty-six-year-old *Southampton* will depart from Queens under Captain Thomas Hinley of Whitestone, while the *Pennsylvania* will simultaneously leave 34th Street with Captain Will Schow of Elmhurst at the wheel.

But only one boat, the *Southampton*, is in service on that final day. Back and forth it plies all afternoon, each trip with but a handful of passengers. Borden Avenue, which only a few years before had been clogged with city traffic, is alone and silent. The neighborhood has a sorry, deserted feeling since so many have moved away. Miller's Hotel? The building that had once been the busy hotel is now a warehouse. A small ornate structure with the words "Queens County Bank" is now part of a coal yard. A truck rattles by once in a while; three trolleys idle on Front Street, waiting to start their route at the appointed time.

Barred are the wide entrances to the ferry house. Admission is through a small door. The passenger who pays the nickel fare slips into the waiting room. A tiger cat lies curled asleep in a passageway where thousands of hurrying feet had trod in years gone before. A newsstand, candy counter

Ferryboat going into the terminal. *Greater Astoria Historical Society.*

and possibly a soda fountain are boarded up, perhaps for years. There are ghostly spirits in the center of the room. There is a rumor that the terminal and docks are to be torn down the very next day.

That last trip carries no curiosity passengers, mostly just relatives and friends of employees. A red fire glows from every pole in the ship's stern. In maritime tradition, it is a signal of sorrow—a clanking of chains. The boat begins its last trip to Manhattan and arrives without incident. A couple of passengers depart into the darkness. Somewhere in the dusk and the distance, an unseen bell is tolling a knell.

A red fire glows, a distant bell tolls and the 34th Street Ferry pulls off for the final time—its last seven-minute trip to Queens. As the boat churns out of its Manhattan slip, a small group of men grown gray in its service watches the waves and the light-studded buildings recede. One doffs his hat and sadly says, "Goodbye, goodbye." Men who devoted their lives to these boats are making history themselves by taking the final run. The longest serving, Thomas Milling of 12th Street, Long Island City, was an engineer for forty-five years. Ole Olson, a night watchman, worked for four decades.

The ferry is an institution rich in memories, carrying a multitude on each load. Among them were the racetrack crowd, beach and picnic groups, more staid community throngs and sober soldiers in khaki. On that last trip, it carries only twenty-three passengers, two horse-drawn wagons and one motor truck.

It docks. An iron gate rattles open. The whistle screeches a swan song. The two horses, whose ears cock forward at the surprise of the prolonged shrill of whistles, now steel themselves to their task and drag their carts to the streets. The motor vehicle chugs a moment and then silently ascends the incline. The little group of passengers heads for the two red trolleys that are standing empty at the terminal.

The Hunter's Point Ferry is now a part of history.

Chapter 46

THE BROTHERHOOD OF PULLMAN PORTERS

*O*ne of the neat things about history is to go through something old, like a diary or a newspaper, and come across a story that today might be obscure but adds a new dimension to our community and whose significance goes far beyond something local.

Before interstate highways and jet travel, long-distance trips were by train, and as they often took days, an accommodation was set up. Pullman Sleeper Cars, named after George Pullman, were a luxurious way to sleep and rest on long journeys. A special team of men, almost exclusively African American, staffed these cars. Pullman porters and stewards, often sons of ex-slaves, were world renowned for the excellent service patrons received for travel accommodations. However, if a towel was missing, they had to pay for it out of their pocket. Sometimes, food and travel consumed half of their wages. They could not sleep in the same cars they maintained.

They organized themselves into the International Brotherhood of the Sleeping Car Porters. It was the first union organized by African Americans to receive a charter from the American Federation of Labor. Under the banner "Fight or Be Slaves," the union became a powerful political force. In the early 1930s, it fought and won fierce battles for racial equality. Legendary civil rights leader A. Philip Randolph was its first president.

He's "George" to you if you take your ideas of Pullman travel from the movies, but the veteran of the sleeping coach called his porter Tom or Jason or Wally—or whatever else his actual name happened to be—and profited accordingly. Outside the Pullman Company Porters' Home at 42–18 28th Street, a reporter posed the question of why Pullman porters were all called "George" to a Memphis lad who had just finished a run from Chicago. The

Pullman porter, 1943. *Jack Delano, Farm Security Administration, Library of Congress.*

train was parked in the Pennsylvania Railyard at Sunnyside, and the lad was checking into the company hotel for eight hours of sleep. "I don't know," he said, "perhaps because Mr. Pullman's name was George."

The young man continued, "Traveling salesmen and such who ride the same road all the time get to know the porters by their real names, and some of them are good friends after a while. They don't all call us George." He grinned.

Each week, the porters logged more than 400,000 miles—or 17 times around the Earth at the equator. The Long Island City house may have been the most widely traveled gathering in the country. A 1,000-mile week was on the low end for a Pullman porter. Some men covered as much as 10,000 miles in one month. When the reporter contacted a spokesperson at the railroad regarding this, he got a terse, "No comment." "The company bosses are scared about giving out facts," one of the guests said. "The last time that happened, someone tried to organize the porters."

The home was run as a hotel by a former porter, Jerry Williams, and his wife. The men slept in double bunks, got meals and had a lounge with newspapers from around the country. They also had a radio. From fifty to eighty men slept in two shifts. Every day, a new set of guests would check in. The doors were locked at 11:00 p.m., and late arrivals were not admitted. By 7:00 a.m. the following day, everyone had to be up, and an hour later, new arrivals would be bunking down for the 8:00 a.m. to 4:00 p.m. shift. No porter, unless ill, could spend more than two nights in the house. It was open only to those who did not live in New York.

From as far west as Chicago, and from Miami or New Orleans, and less distant runs on the Pennsylvania system, came the regulars at the Long Island City home. One man made the trip between New York and Miami every week.

"It's summer in Florida on Wednesday and a New York winter on Sundays," he said. "If ever I settle down and remain here, I'd think it's Sunday all winter long, and the whole summer would be one Wednesday, I guess."

Chapter 47

EMPTY CHAIR ON STAGE

*B*ix Beiderbecke and Louis Armstrong both played the cornet and lived in Queens, and although they are often compared to each other, their approach to jazz was markedly different. Armstrong emphasized showmanship; Beiderbecke focused on melody. Armstrong was a stage performer, engaging his audience and soaring into the high registers. The largely self-taught Beiderbecke, lost in exploring classical music and jazz harmonics, stared at his feet during performances.

Leon Bismark "Bix" Beiderbecke (March 10, 1903–August 6, 1931) was an American jazz cornetist, jazz pianist and composer who influenced in one form or another such diverse artists as Bing Crosby and Lester Young. The musicians he worked with, all jazz-era legends themselves, were in awe of Bix's style. One said, "I have never heard a tone like he got before or since. He played every note full, big, rich, and round, with a powerful drive that few white musicians had in those days."

Bing Crosby was quick to attribute Bix and the enormous influence he had on the crooner. "Bix and all the rest would play and exchange ideas on the piano," he said. "I didn't contribute anything, but I listened and learned...and was influenced by these musicians." Clarinetist Pee Wee Russell praised Beiderbecke's ability to drive the band. "He more or less made you play whether you wanted to or not." When Bix was away from the Paul Whiteman orchestra, Whiteman insisted that an empty chair be kept on the stage.

Bix Beiderbecke at Doyle's Academy of Music in Cincinnati, Ohio, 1924. *Public domain, retouched by Hans Eekhoff, scanned from a copy obtained from John Vincent.*

Jazz legend Eddie Condon wrote of being amazed by Beiderbecke's piano playing: "All my life I had been listening to music....But I had never heard anything remotely like what Beiderbecke played." His laidback style showed the way to Bill Evans's cool jazz of the 1950s. Musicians today recognize his work as modern, not so much in style but in attitude.

Beiderbecke taught himself music mainly by ear. His sister recalled that he stood on the floor playing the piano with his hands over his head at two. Five years later, he was the subject of an admiring article in the *Davenport Daily Democrat* that proclaimed, "Seven-year-old boy musical wonder! Little Bickie Beiderbecke plays any selection he hears." His path in life was set when he heard the jazz music off the riverboats that docked in downtown Davenport, Iowa. He ran away from home to be with musicians.

After several bouts of alcoholism, he wrote to his brother, "I'd go to hell to hear a good band."

Alcoholism killed him. Beiderbecke died in his apartment, #1G, 43–30 46th Street, in Sunnyside, Queens, on Thursday, August 6, 1931. He was twenty-eight.

In 2003, to mark the 100th anniversary of his birth, the Greater Astoria Historical Society and other community organizations, spearheaded by Paul Maringelli and the Bix Beiderbecke Sunnyside Memorial Committee, erected a plaque in Beiderbecke's honor at the apartment building in which he died. Looking for some details of his death, we scanned local papers for the month of August 1931. There were stories of yachting in Bayside and social events in Little Neck. Vacation itineraries for local politicians and pastors were carefully spelled out. The pages were filled with a host of names once notable but now obscure.

But not a word, a hint, not a shadow of Bix could be found.

After almost one hundred years, when jazz artists gather and talk among themselves, they still try to define his influence on them and their art. Each year, when someone hears his music for the first time, his fan base grows. As the decades passed, he climbed to the pinnacle of his art. He has become immortal.

So how do we understand Bix?

"I tried to explain Bix to the gang," songwriter Hoagy Carmichael once wrote, "but it was no good, like the telling of a vivid, personal dream.... The emotion couldn't be transmitted." Years later, Eddie Condon painted his friend as only a fellow artist could: "Bix took out a silver cornet. He put it to his lips and blew a phrase. The sound [that] came out was like a girl saying yes."

Chapter 48

THE ARCHITECT
OF GREAT BRIDGES

*T*he Triborough Bridge is an engineering triumph, a model of urban planning, a "traffic machine" that many regard as having never been equaled since it opened in 1936. In November 2008, the Triborough Bridge was officially renamed after Robert F. Kennedy at the request of the Kennedy family. No problem, as New York City has renamed more than one thousand locations for similar reasons.

The real issue is, who should be honored as the "father" of the Triborough Bridge?

Was it Robert Moses, the "master builder" of twentieth-century New York? Perhaps it was Othmar Ammann, who gets credit as the architect for several major bridges in the city. Or should it be an audit clerk who once worked at the Motor Vehicle Bureau, Queens's own George A. Haupt?

Haupt's tale is a strange story indeed, for it is of dreams unfulfilled and numbing, lousy luck. The *Long Island Star-Journal* did a profile on him in 1939. Some say his story was fiction, an offhand filler that editors will throw into a paper on a slow news day. Others are not so sure, as the article in question has a sad-looking older man holding up a model of the Triborough made of boxes and string—just the sort of thing a schoolkid would make for a show-and-tell project.

It was three years after the bridge's opening day, and the old man was still bitter over not being invited to sit on the reviewing stand with dignitaries. He groused, "Only the big fellows get the glory. The little fellow is never mentioned. Mr. Moses said, 'It doesn't matter who first suggested the bridge

Triborough Bridge postcard, 1936. *Greater Astoria Historical Society.*

or who had the first idea for the bridge—the main thing is that we have it.' Well, that burned me up because the matter of who first got the idea for the bridge seems rather important to me!"

You see, Haupt claimed that the bridge was his idea. When he was a young deckhand who worked on the ferry that ran between the House of Refuge for Boys on Randall's Island, the state hospital on Ward's Island and Harlem Hospital at 120th Street, it came to him.

Onboard, he met both Captain Barger, responsible for the House of Refuge, and Dr. Gustave Scholar, head of the medical staff on Ward's Island. They told him stories of poor people from the Bronx and Queens who had to travel, as they said, "halfway around the world" to 120th Street for a boat to go to their jobs or see their relatives on the islands.

So the young man got to thinking about a bridge and began to idly make sketches. In 1909, years before there was any talk of a Triborough Bridge, Haupt made a little plaster model of his idea and gave it to Harlem alderman Percy Davis. It showed the now-classic three spans converging on Randall's Island—not much different in design and concept from what was built a generation later. Young George's idea created quite a stir in the community.

Unfortunately, as often happens to be politicians, Alderman Davis got into "trouble" and had to leave town rather quickly. No one knows what happened to George's plans.

Enter Gustav Lindenthal, builder of both the Queensboro and Hell Gate Bridges. Haupt met Lindenthal when they were both members of the Harlem Maennerchor, a sizeable German singing club. Haupt discussed the ideas with Lindenthal. The bridge builder liked his suggestions. It was probably not a coincidence for this story that Othmar Ammann, who later built the Triborough Bridge, was Lindenthal's assistant.

George Haupt went on with his life. He moved to Queens in 1921 when his East 120th Street home was torn down for a school. He got a small job with the city.

A few years later, he heard plans to build a great bridge that would link the three boroughs. Excited that his idea might finally find some interest, George painstakingly reconstructed his old model with the home-spun materials at hand. The Manhattan approach was a piece of felt from a stamp pad. The towers and Little Hell Gate span came from cigar boxes. He shaped a piece of copper stripping to form the long span over the East River. Cables were fashioned from lead wire. A lawyer friend would show it to Nathan Burkan, a well-connected celebrity attorney—and one of the Triborough Bridge commissioners.

Just days before George was to meet him, Commissioner Burkan suddenly and unexpectedly died. George never did get a chance to show his model to anyone that mattered.

Years later, the newspaper tracked him down. The pictures show a dejected-looking Haupt, sitting next to his bridge model, going through a scrapbook full of yellowed letters and forgotten testimonials that complimented him on his foresight. After the bridge was built, the heartbroken old man frequently walked up to Astoria to look at "his" bridge.

For the man who told anyone who would listen that he was the "father of the Triborough Bridge," there was an official recognition of sorts on its opening day. After Haupt politely wrote to Mayor LaGuardia asking to be invited to the ceremonies, the mayor graciously sent him a copy of the program.

Chapter 49

THE MATCH KING

"Every picture tells a story," sang Rod Stewart in 1971. In Long Island City, it seems every building has a story of someone's dream—perhaps delivering a unique commodity, revolutionizing a new industrial process or simply making an old hat into an item new and wonderful. When someone said, "A city is not gauged by its length and width, but by the boldness of its vision and the height of its dreams," they were probably thinking of Long Island City.

It all started when a gentleman was curious about the backstory of one of his properties. His thinking was that he could promote its future by gleaming something unique from its past. He knew it was a match factory. So from that little nugget tumbled out this fascinating story of a clever man and the humble matchbook.

Once at the fringes of Burden's Marsh, the property was rebranded as Queens Plaza when the Queensboro Bridge was built through its center. A worthless patch of the bog was suddenly the most sought-after land in Queens. Almost immediately, the Queensboro Elevated Train connected the area to the rest of the city, and commercial loft buildings arose just south of Bridge Plaza. Starting in the 1920s and continuing for the next decade, the Lion Match Company built and expanded its factory at 22–15 43rd Avenue. It is, in a sense, a monument to one man's dream. Meet Leo Greenbaum.

His 1950 *New York Times* obituary explored the path of a thirteen-year-old German immigrant who was to be a bootblack, dishwasher, waiter and restaurant owner over the next six decades. When he died at age seventy-

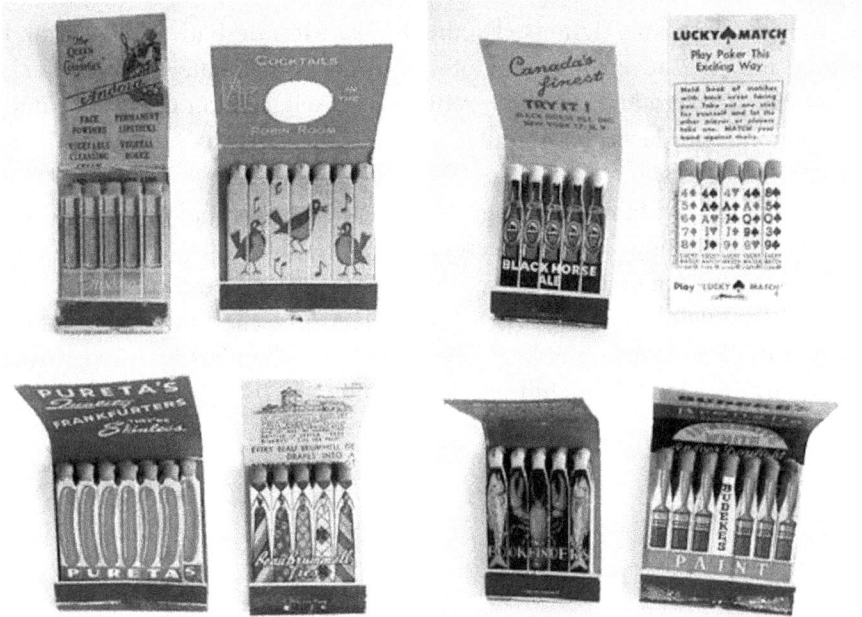

Lion matchbook. *Public domain.*

four, he was a resident of Central Park West and a member of the Elks, Masons and the Harmony and Metropolis Country Clubs. His son, Monroe, was a graduate of the Ivy League's Dartmouth College.

In 1917, Leo started manufacturing paper matches with one secondhand machine on the Lower East Side. He later moved his factory to Brooklyn and, in 1924, to Long Island City, where the business ultimately expanded into three large buildings. Leo was a mover and a shaker within the matchbook industry, with twenty-one patents. Not afraid to gamble on new lines and new ideas, he was called the "Match King" by admirers and competitors alike.

Among matchbook collectors (called phillumenists), the Lion Match name is legendary. "The Matchcover Vault," a resource for matchbook collectors, sums up Lion Match's place in history: "There's nothing like holding an old Lion full-book 'Feature' in the palm of your hand. You notice right away that it's not like any other cover. It's heavier; it's thicker, and you know when you open it up that it's going to be a veritable feast for the eyes (sigh!)."

When Leo's son Monroe took over in the 1950s, the world began to change: on the horizon were both the surgeon general's Report on Smoking as well as disposable lighters. By the 1960s, Monroe had sold Lion and moved into the advertising part of the business. Ultimately, Lion Match moved to Chicago and, in 1988, rebranding itself as Lion Circle, got into promotional products. Its manufacturing equipment was purchased by a firm in Honduras.

And the Lion Match Building? Now managed and majority-owned by the Werwaiss family, who has been in Long Island City for more than one hundred years, the building has recently been renovated and converted into a multi-tenant loft building. With Long Island City in another ascending cycle, the Lion Match Building's future seems as limitless as when it was owned by the Match King himself, Mr. Greenbaum.

Chapter 50

LAST OF THE VAMPS

Thank you to grandson Jack Tissot for information on Emile E. Tissot and other members of his family.

T he professional Long Island City Fire Department was formed in the early 1890s. When Queens County joined Greater New York in 1898, it was the only force in the borough accepted as full professionals by the New York Fire Department. The borough's other companies were regarded as "volunteer companies," or more commonly "vamps," an expression from olden times that meant to tramp or walk. Volunteer firemen generally went to fires on foot, dragging their equipment with long ropes.

Emile A. Tissot, who is profiled in this piece, was a member (in the 1880s) of Long Island City's earlier volunteer force. He sat down, at ninety-three, for this interview in 1954. He lived for seventy-two years on one block in Astoria before moving into his son's house in Flushing. Tissot was the last living Long Island City volunteer fireman.

The reporter wrote that the old gent started with a twinkle in his eye: "When I was a lad, we boys herded the cows out to pasture every morning— and drove them back every night. There were dirt roads then and no law against keeping cows [in Long Island City]."

Tissot continued:

> *I started out in the hardware business when I was 15—at $2 a week. In 1883 I joined the Astoria Hook and Ladder Company Number 1 of the*

LIC veteran firemen and apparatus. *Greater Astoria Historical Society.*

Long Island City Fire Department. My mother didn't like me to go to the fires at night. When the alarm sounded, she wouldn't wake me up if I was sleeping. But any fireman who didn't answer it was fined—$1 for a real fire and 50 cents for a false alarm—so I managed to get to most of them.

He downplayed the risks of firefighting:

We didn't have many fires during the five years I was on active duty in the department because Astoria was very small. But you should have seen us when there was one....We'd run to the firehouse just as fast as we knew how. When there, we grabbed the hook and ladder truck and started pulling, with the rest of them following along behind. Didn't have a horse to pull it...too expensive to feed 'em.

Sometimes we'd have to pull that wagon as far as Bowery Bay or North Beach—a big summer resort when I was a youth. It used to be dancing pavilions and amusements—but you'd get run over by a jet if you tried to waltz over there now. That's where they built LaGuardia Airport.

When the city took over the Long Island City Fire Department after the 1898 consolidation, there were 150 members of the Veterans Firemen's

Association. In about 1945, they sold their firehouse to the American Legion. The association continued to meet until 1950, when there were only three members left. When Tissot was interviewed in 1954, he was the last person who could lay claim to having witnessed the things he shared with us.

He passed away in 1958.

The old volunteer firemen are all dead; their heroic deeds are long forgotten. Their only memorial is a short paragraph in a newspaper announcing a death. But suppose magnanimous courage is human nature's noblest quality. In that case, the day will come when the unsung hero—whether a fireman, a policeman or a soldier who risks their life to serve our nation—will inherit the immortality of fame.

This is Emile Tissot's entry into that roster.

PART IV

LIC:
Cradle of Creativity
(from 1960)

Chapter 51

THE FIRST PAGE

History can be found in the most mundane of settings.
—*Kevin Walsh, of Forgotten NY*

*F*or example, take a second-floor apartment at a three-story walkup on the corner of Broadway and 37th Street. Over the years, 32–05 37th Street was a beauty parlor, a dentist's office and the lab of Chester Carlson, where he invented the photocopier on a Saturday in October 1938.

Long Island City may be extraordinary in its dining, exciting in its growing arts scene and legendary in its industrial past. Still, all stem from a common source: it is the home of creative people. Here is but one story.

Chester was a curious child interested in various topics: graphic arts, chemistry, the very how and why of things. He put these interests together as an adult; as a patent attorney, he was faced with the task of duplicating paperwork in filing patents at work. He found that other than using carbon paper, mimeograph machines or retyping, it was impossible to quickly and cheaply reproduce documents.

It is said that the inventor's instinct is to travel the uncharted course, and recalling his interests of childhood, Carlson turned to the little-known field of photoconductivity. After reading everything he could find on the topic, he experimented with a witch's brew of chemicals.

After abortive attempts in his Jackson Heights kitchen (and angering his wife after accidentally setting several fires), he moved his lab to a storage room in her mother's beauty parlor on 37th Street in Astoria. He hired a German refugee, Otto Kornei, to help him.

"10.-22.-38
ASTORIA." First
photocopy. *Xerox
Corporation.*

We have Carlson's account of their moment of success: "I went to the lab that day, and Otto had a freshly-prepared sulfur coating on a zinc plate. [He] took a glass microscope slide and printed on it '10.-22.-38 ASTORIA' with ink.

"We pulled down the shade to make the room as dark as possible, then he rubbed the sulfur surface vigorously with a handkerchief to apply an electrostatic charge, laid the slide on the surface, and placed the combination under a bright incandescent lamp for a few seconds. The slide was then removed, and a powder was sprinkled on its surface. Then, by gently blowing off the loose powder, there was a near-perfect duplicate of the [image]...on the glass slide." It was the world's first photocopy.

"Both of us repeated the experiment several times to convince ourselves that it was true, then we made some permanent copies by transferring the powder images to wax paper and heating the sheets to melt the wax. Then we went out to lunch and to celebrate."

On October 6, 1942, the Patent Office issued Carlson's patent on electrophotography. "I knew," he said, "that I had a very big idea by the tail, but could I tame it?" Chester Carlson, who experimented in an Astoria storeroom, invented the photocopier. He obtained a patent in 1940—one of twenty-eight he earned in his lifetime.

He approached several corporations, but new commercial inventions were of little interest, with the nation soon at war. Even the National Inventors Council dismissed his work. "I became discouraged," he later reminisced, "and several times decided to drop the idea completely. But each time, I returned to try again. Finally, I was thoroughly convinced that the invention was too promising to be dormant."

In 1944, he finally caught the attention of Battelle Development Corporation, an entity whose purpose was to sponsor new inventions. It, in turn, partnered with the Haloid Company of Rochester, New York, a manufacturer of paper. Rejecting cumbersome *electrophotography*, the word Carlson had coined, Battelle, after it reached out to a Greek-speaking professor who taught the classics at Ohio State, coined *Xerography*, meaning "dry writing" in Greek. It was shortened to *Xerox*.

The first commercially successful photocopier, the Xerox 914, arrived in 1959. After that, Haloid renamed itself the Xerox Corporation. Its website states, "They saw enormous potential where others saw only the hazards."

A biographer wrote, "Carlson had lived inside himself as a lonely workaholic. His parents fell ill when he was young. From age 13, he worked to help support his desperately poor family and put himself through school. He managed to graduate from Cal. Tech during the Depression, and then struggled to stay employed while poverty swirled about him."

Carlson earned an estimated $150 million ($950 million today). He gave two-thirds of it to charity, becoming one of the great philanthropists of the twentieth century. He told his wife he wanted "to die a poor man." In 1968, sixty-two-year-old Chester Carlson took in a movie one afternoon with a few hours between meetings. He died of a heart attack watching images flowing on a screen.

"To know Chester Carlson was to like him, to love him, and to respect him…as a man of exceptional moral stature and as a humanist," stated United Nations secretary general U Thant at Carlson's memorial service in Rochester.

Money wasn't the point for Carlson. He had finally succeeded in his struggle to gain self-acceptance and to make reproducible the images that danced in his head. He left an enduring maxim: "You are successful the moment you start moving toward a worthwhile goal."

A philosopher once observed that Carlson "built a fifty-year bridge from an old world of typewriters and carbon paper into a new world yet to come… one where paper is only an archival backup and daily commerce moves…to our digital screens." The floodgates of information were opened.

The world will produce upward of three trillion xerographic copies this year. Astoria's name will forever be on the "First Page of the Information Age."

Chapter 52

AN AMERICAN ODYSSEY

*O*dysseus was the hero of an epic poem, *Odyssey*, which is the sequel to another work, *The Iliad*. Both stories from ancient Greece are the oldest written works in literature. The word *odyssey* means to take a long, wandering journey, often fraught with adventure if not danger, encountering inimitable people as you pass through extraordinary settings.

A weekly Friday night program on television, *Route 66*, was a direct descendant of the genre. It aired on CBS from 1960 to 1964. Although its name invoked the legendary highway, the mythic "Main Street of America" encouraged a generation to travel the actual Route 66; it was filmed at locations across the country.

Buz Murdock (played by George Maharis) was a "hard-slugging guy from Hell's Kitchen," and his partner, Tod Stiles (played by Martin Milner), a "preppy fellow that had just inherited a Corvette," made for an unlikely team. Fueled with a shared wanderlust for adventure, the series chronicled their four-year odyssey across America.

A critic marveled, "The idea of traveling without a destination, helping people in need and working for gas, lodging, and food to get to the next place, seems so American and adventuresome." These odd jobs often brought them in contact with whatever storyline was at the center of that week's epic. A reviewer stated, "It was an attempt to blend the closed-off, social-issues-based storytelling of the best anthology dramas, with the recurring characters of a more traditional drama series."

Logo for *Route 66* TV series. *Vectored by FOX 52,* Route 66 *DVD, public domain.*

Tod and Buz were cast as a kind of "roving Greek chorus," witnesses to every shade of the human condition—the rich and poor, old and young, drifters who time had passed by, residents of the gutter and prisoners in gilded drawing rooms—but all facing plot lines that forced them to encounter challenges within their lives.

And like the original Odysseus, Astoria native Maharis was also Greek. Now retired after an acting career that spanned more than seventy credits (and an Emmy nomination for his role in the series), he reflects back on the show that launched his career: "It was about two men who were trying to catch a star and find a place in this world."

Maharis continued, "We worked six days a week, sometimes seven, because we were always behind schedule. You got up at 5 in the morning, and you get back to your motel at 7 or 9 at night, sometimes even later. We did 32 to 35 shows a year. Now, they do 20 to 22, at most. No one would try anything like that today." The pace of twelve- to fifteen-hour workdays ultimately endangered his health and forced him to leave the show. Without his chemistry, it soon ended.

Hallmarks of the series included its soaring dialogue and the ways it introduced viewers to new ways of life and new cultures. It was one of the most unique and memorable programs on television or, as reviewers later dubbed it, "artistic TV" or "seat-of-pants television." It was a chapter from the early years before the medium fell into set-piece dramas and tame scripts. Filmed in black-and-white, the American landscape was mid-twentieth century yet also oddly full of people and plot lines that would fit easily in the twenty-first century. Its dozens of characters helped break the color barrier, and at the century's midpoint, it showcased the legends from the century's first half and those future stars still around to this day.

"It was very, very interesting," Maharis continued, "because no matter where you went, every town had its own personality. It was totally different from the other town you went to, even if it was only 50 to 60 miles away. Of course, that's not true anymore. You can go a thousand miles now, and everyone's wearing the same clothes, singing the same songs, eating the same food."

Chapter 53

AN ARTIST OF TWO WORLDS

Isamu Noguchi's father was Japanese, and his mother was American. Instead of this being a source of confusion and uncertainty, it enabled him to be a citizen of each world. He could seamlessly draw from both and create a fusion with the best that each had to offer.

> *You can find out how to do something and then do it…or do something and then find out what you did.*

In traditional Japanese culture, there is a keen sense of seeing the beauty of art in nature. Noguchi's wide range of talents echoes this as he examined ceramics, ink painting, woodworking and, of course, sculpture.

> *We are a landscape of all we have seen.*

Noguchi, who went to school in Indiana, identified as a Hoosier for the rest of his life. However, his spirit of adventure and curiosity stamped his personality unquestionably as American.

> *I am always learning, always discovering. Art should become as one with its surroundings.*

Isamu Noguchi in Tokyo, 1951, photo by Jun Miki. *Public domain.*

Over the next sixty years, he traveled around the world in constant motion, absorbing experiences, learning with each level of experience a new understanding of the myriad forms of human expression.

When an artist stopped being a child, he would stop being an artist.

His endless search for the foundations of modern art and vast knowledge in so many spheres of his discipline were seldom matched and, most likely, never will be surpassed.

Everything is sculpture. Any material, any idea without hindrance born into space, I consider sculpture.

He hit his stride when he moved into work with rock, primarily with granite and basalt. In that medium, Noguchi felt that he could convey something that was permanent and immortal.

In my work, I wanted something irreducible, an absence of the gimmicky and clever.

Most of his life held one constant: movement. He traveled from one atelier to the next, having work rejected as often as it was lauded. Between major gigs, he did portraiture, drawing on his vast knowledge to move ever forward into his art, his passion.

I perceive my limitations even as work. There are times when I see nothing but restrictions, barriers. Learning takes time.

In 1961, he moved to Long Island City and purchased space for a museum in 1974. After renovations, he opened the location as the Noguchi Museum in 1985. He died in 1988.

The respected art critic behind publicdelivery.org summed up his work and the man: "The blend of Western and Eastern cultures, modern and traditional life, organic and geometric alignment of nature are some of the efforts Isamu Noguchi made to create tranquility in his work."

To order space is to give it meaning. Appreciate the moment.

Chapter 54

"I ONCE LOVED A GIRL"—A DYLAN LYRIC

*I*t was an iconic image: a musician walks through slush and fading winter light down Jones Street toward West 4th in the Village with a pretty girl at his side. Upstairs, his sixty-dollar-a-month apartment has a few pieces of secondhand furniture. On his back is a coat too thin for the cold; on his arm is his first great love. At the corner, a Volkswagen bus.

Say hello to twenty-one-year-old Bob Dylan of Hibbing, Minnesota, and nineteen-year-old Suze Rotolo of Sunnyside, Queens.

From the cover of *The Freewheelin' Bob Dylan*, this image was an iconic moment from 1963 that launched an iconoclastic age. More than five decades have passed, yet there is scarcely a young person brimming with excitement, ready to explore the future at their feet, who does not see themselves reflected in that couple.

Wikipedia states the facts: Susan Elizabeth Rotolo was Dylan's girlfriend from 1961 to 1964. Her parents, members of the American Communist Party, moved from Brooklyn to Sunnyside. In June 1960, she graduated from Bryant High School in Astoria. About the time she met Dylan, she was working as a political activist in the office of the Congress of Racial Equality (CORE).

Describing their meeting in his memoir, *Chronicles, Volume One*, Dylan wrote:

> *Right from the start, I couldn't take my eyes off her. We started talking, and my head started to spin. Cupid's arrow had whistled past my ears before, but this time it hit me in the heart, and the weight of it dragged me*

The Freewheelin' Bob Dylan album. *Robert Singleton music collection, original may belong to Columbia Records.*

overboard....She had a smile that could light up a street full of people and was extremely lively, had a kind of voluptuousness—a Rodin sculpture come to life.

Columnist Nat Hentoff wrote that "at the time of this album's release, Dylan is growing at a swift, experience-hungry rate." Dylan later acknowledged Suze's strong influence on his music and art during that period. Elizabeth Mitchell of the *New York Daily News* reveals that Suze played a vital role in developing Dylan's career, and the seeds she sowed led to the ultimate destruction of their relationship. "It was not until they met," states Mitchell, "that Dylan's writing began to address issues such as the civil rights movement and the threat of nuclear war."

Decades later, Rotolo disclosed that "Bob was charismatic: he was a beacon, a lighthouse, he was also a black hole. He required committed backup and protection I was unable to provide consistently, probably because I needed them myself....I was unable to find solid ground. I was on quicksand and very vulnerable."

After living together for several years, they started to drift apart. Shortly after moving into her sister's apartment on Avenue B, Suze discovered she was pregnant with Dylan's first child. She and Dylan agreed to an abortion, an operation that was performed when such procedures were illegal.

Mitchell writes:

The building where Dylan once lived for $60 a month was sold in 2015 for $6 million. The [album] cover image has vanished as the original photo negative disappeared from the Columbia files. And what of the eyewitnesses to that February day? Suze Rotolo died of lung cancer in 2011. Photographer Don Hunstein died in March 2017 after suffering from Alzheimer's disease.

And Dylan? He's not talking.

Chapter 55

GO ASK ALLIS

I do not foresee that atomic energy is to be a great boon for a long time. I have to say that for the present, it is a menace. Perhaps it is well that it should be.
—*Albert Einstein*

We do not choose our problems; we do not choose our products; we are pushed, we are forced—by what? By a system which has no purpose and goal transcending it, and which makes man its appendix.
—*Erich Fromm*

*A*t Ravenswood, on the East River, within the heart of a city of eight million, Con Edison once proposed to build the world's largest nuclear power plant. Its capacity, one thousand megawatts, was to be equal to all the atomic plants in the United States at that time. Advocates of nuclear energy were sanguine, touting it as an inexhaustible source of clean energy without the dangers of air pollution from fossil fuels. It was called "Big Allis."

But for most, the word *nuclear* has the taint of fearsome images from Nagasaki and Hiroshima and ominous mushroom clouds in the Nevada desert or Bikini Atoll.

When Con Edison and Westinghouse announced, in December 1962, plans for a nuclear reactor in Ravenswood, the first public meeting on February 19, 1963, at St. Rita's Church drew hundreds of people. However,

Ravenswood Generating Station in Long Island City viewed from Roosevelt Island. *Rhododendrites (Creative Commons BY-SA 4.0).*

they quickly made up their minds in opposition when they heard that nuclear industry standards mandated various population exclusion zones around reactors measured miles and not, as with Ravenswood, a few hundred feet.

It was a meeting that would inaugurate the nation's first public protest against nuclear power facilities. Hearings were duly conducted over the next year. At city hall, State Senator Seymour Thaler (D-Queens) told city council, "The mind of man has not yet invented an accident-proof piece of mechanical equipment." Queens Borough president Mario J. Cariello voiced the community's sentiments, stating, "I am opposed, and I will continue in that stand until convinced otherwise."

The utility's chairman, Harland C. Forbes, responded to their comments: "It seems to me that the public, in general, has reached the point where it has accepted nuclear plants as a matter of course." He further stated that he would have no objection to "building a nuclear reactor in Times Square as for that matter."

When David Lilienthal, first chairman of the Atomic Energy Commission, opined at a Senate-House Atomic Energy Commission hearing that he wouldn't dream of living in Queens if the plant were built, resistance grew. He was immediately slammed by Chairman John Pastore (D-Rhode Island), who condemned Lilienthal's comments for speaking "rather loosely" and called his criticism—that the government backed the atomic industry—"very unfair."

The chorus of voices hostile to Con Ed's proposed Ravenswood nuclear reactor continued to grow. The comments included the possibility of sabotage, the possible pollution of the East River by the plant, the accidental emissions of atomic waste and contamination of food manufacturers and processing plants in Long Island City.

Opponents argued that these and other fears would discourage people from becoming Queens residents. They darkly hinted it would retard the borough's development. That point won the argument. Con Ed announced that it would purchase electricity from Canada. The Ravenswood nuclear reactor was dead.

Chapter 56

THE WOMAN WHO LOVED WORDS

O n March 21, 1951, Fed Astaire hosted the twenty-third Academy Awards at the legendary RKO Pantages Theatre before an audience of Hollywood legends. Nominees for Best Actress included Gloria Swanson (*Sunset Boulevard*), Anne Baxter and Bette Davis (*All About Eve*). The award went to Judy Holliday for her performance as Billie Dawn in *Born Yesterday*. The *New York Times* called her performance "not only funny but also human and moving."

Judy Holliday was raised in Sunnyside Gardens. She was born in 1921 literally into show business; her mother, a piano teacher, went into labor while at a play. Throughout her life, people close to her were notable in the arts. Her father, Abe, was the president of the American Federation of Musicians. Her husband, David Oppenheim, was dean of the NYU Tisch School of the Arts; and her son Jonathan was a noted film editor.

Her first job was in Orson Welles's Mercury Theater as a switchboard operator. Next, she worked in a Greenwich Village troupe with Leonard Bernstein, Betty Comden and Adolph Green. Then, after a brief stint in Hollywood at Fox Studios, where she stood up to mogul Darryl F. Zanuck's aggressive sexual overtures, the tough New Yorker returned home to Broadway. As was customary at the time, she ditched her birth name, Yamin Tuvim, in favor of Judy Holliday for a stage name. "Holy Days" is one of the Hebrew meanings of *tuvim*.

In 1945, her first Broadway role, in *Kiss Them for Me*, won her the Clarence Derwent Award for best supporting actress. The musical *Bells Are Ringing*

Publicity photo of Judy Holliday. *Public domain.*

earned her the New York Drama Desk Award and the Tony Award (chosen over Ethel Merman and Julie Andrews). The exceptional performance of the young actress in the stage version of *Adam's Rib* (1949) prompted director George Cukor and stars Katharine Hepburn and Spencer Tracy to convince producer Harry Cohn of Holliday's marketability for the film version.

Critics state that Holliday's acting career was "brief but impressive. Her canon is relatively small, including five Broadway shows." Yet among Broadway performers, she remains a legend. "I knew people who knew her and had only praise for her as a talent and person, as well," states Broadway star Donna McKechnie (*A Chorus Line*). That impression is echoed by producer Gene Kirkwood (*Rocky*), who is making a movie of Holliday titled *Smart Blonde*. Kirkwood said, "Judy Holliday's story is for the ages and yet so relatable within the context of today."

Yet despite this success, her career stalled. When she was young, signing some leftist petitions (her parents were Socialists) prompted a congressional committee to summon her to Washington for questioning. Despite an IQ of 172 (and being equally adept at comedy and drama), she was typecast as a squeaky-voiced "dumb blonde." Her career stagnated.

She tried singing. She considered getting behind the camera and writing scripts. Her frustration was evident when she stated, "I've always loved words. I ate up all the books I could get my hands on, and when I couldn't get books, I read candy wrappers and labels on cereal and toothpaste boxes."

The stress perhaps contributed to a diagnosis of cancer in her late thirties. Her last public performance, in 1965, was near her roots where she started, at a café in the Village. One of the songs she sang that evening was "The Party's Over." A week later, at forty-three, she was dead.

Chapter 57

WE ARE BUILDING
A PIANO FOREVER

alking into the Steinway Piano factory, you notice the fragrance of wood, be it Sitka spruce from the Pacific Northwest, poplar from the Piedmont of the Southeast or rock maple from the Maritimes of Canada. Next, you will pick up the scents of such exotic veneers as Indian apple and mahogany, Macassar ebony and cherry and East Indian rosewood. Then, scattered across the floor are the shavings and dust from ten thousand parts and scores of instruments, each crafted by hand, carefully fit by eye and approved by the smile of a master craftsman.

It is 1972. The brothers Steinway, Henry, John and Theodore, sit down to look at their family's legacy. It is the closing of an era, for they are soon to forever relinquish their family's control over a tradition that has endured the passing of time and the change of generations.

The Steinways are soon to sell their company.

The brothers, as was the family custom, "worked at the bench," as they called their years as apprentices learning every inch of the plant. It was perhaps a lesson for us, too, that, despite the legacy of being born a Steinway—a name in music that resonates with immortals such as Mozart, Bach or Beethoven—their style was understated. They answer their phones at desks that sit among others in the office. Henry shrugs, "Why would I not answer my phone?" and when a glass-enclosed room with a desk is pointed out to brother John, he responds, "Oh, I wouldn't enjoy that; we leave it to our sales manager."

They reflect on their work and their family.

Henry, John and Theodore Steinway. *Henry Steinway Collection, Greater Astoria Historical Society.*

When their father, Theodore E. Steinway, presented a Steinway piano to the White House, he used the occasion to symbolize the sentiment of an American immigrant: "[This is a tribute of thanks to the American nation] from a family who arrived on these friendly shores from abroad, were permitted to seek and make their homes, live their lives, and pursue their work with happiness and contentment."

Commenting on the Steinway Mansion (which as of 2016 was sitting empty, hidden behind warehouses), the brothers mention that their father had a room in the tower "where he could look out over the water" of the East River and Bowery Bay.

The apprentice system, brought from Germany in the mid-nineteenth century, was still used at the plant. Workers on the factory floor share the commitment of the Steinway family. Some even point out beautiful tools once belonging to their grandfathers that are still in use.

The Steinways fully believe that the heart of the operation is the craftsmen on the shop floor. It is where "a skilled man's time should be used for skilled work! Richness of tone, excellent judgment, the balance of volume make our product a sensitive, highly prized instrument," one brother mused.

John Steinway sums up the family's philosophy with a few words from Goethe's *Faust*: "What you have inherited from your forebears, work at it and enjoy it."

Chapter 58

THE HEART OF ART

Transistor: A small electronic device containing a semiconductor and having at least three electrical contacts, used in a circuit as an amplifier, detector or switch.

*A*rtists often use tools that would have been familiar to the ancients—a plectrum hitting strings of a prehistoric harp creates music in many ways similar to a modern Steinway pianist at the keyboard. Likewise, a stone was shaped into sculptured art by mallet and chisel for both a nameless Neolithic artist and Isamu Noguchi.

The transistor revolutionized the creative arts. For the first time since the mists of antiquity, the boundary of artistic expression became limitless. An invisible spark could conjure visions of sight and dimensions of sound and expand the bounds of imagination previously unthinkable.

Masaru Ibuka and Akio Morita co-founded a ragtag Japanese company whose first effort was to miserably fail at making rice cookers in the ruins of postwar Japan. Ibuka, after doing research, had an opportunity to secure the licensing of the transistor technology in the mid-1950s. The transistor, outside of military applications, was primarily used for hearing aids.

In 1957, using transistors, they manufactured the first pocket-sized radio and renamed themselves Sony (homophonic "Sounds Nice") Corporation. After going international, they leased in 1960 a nondescript building on Van Dam Street in Sunnyside, where they created Sony Corporation of America, informally dubbed SONAM.

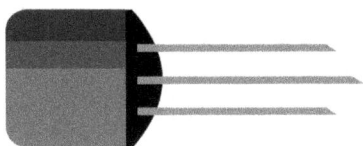

A model of a transistor. *Public domain.*

The launching of SONAM was also the start of a revolution for the entertainment industry: first transistor television (1960), first transistor VTR (1961), Trinitron TV (1968), first compact cassette recorder (1969). Although they lost the Betamax war, they dominated and innovated consumer electronics with the legendary Walkman (1979).

A Wiki entry summarized their success: "Sony has historically been notable for creating its own in-house standards for new recording and storage technologies, instead of adopting those of other manufacturers." Within a scant generation, as they were riding on a curve of creative energy, one historian would state, "They went on to create and deliver more entertainment experiences to more people than anyone else on earth."

By the mid-1980s, when SONAM outgrew its Van Dam address, they were well on the way to becoming one of the world's great entertainment conglomerates. What followed was a whirlwind of acquisitions, including the legendary Columbia Pictures and CBS Records. In doing so, SONAM notched another example of our community's outsized role in creativity and imagination.

For the fiscal year ending March 31, 2020, Sony recorded consolidated annual sales of approximately US $76.67 billion. Its workforce was about 114,400.

All from a bit of transistor, the beating heart of today's art.

Chapter 59

SHE'S OK IF YOU LIKE TALENT

*E*thel Agnes Zimmerman was born in the third-floor bedroom of her grandmother's house at 359 4ᵗʰ Avenue (near 33ʳᵈ Street and 36ᵗʰ Avenue) in Astoria, Queens. A local paper mentioned a reunion at PS 4 in Dutch Kills in December 1913. After the guest speaker gave a talk, a handsome bouquet of roses was presented to her by Miss Ethel Zimmerman, age eight, who later entertained with song and dance in costume. This was the first documented public performance of Ethel Merman.

I take a breath when I have to.

Ethel's parents, Edward and Agnes, always encouraged her love of singing and saw that she got a solid education, including thorough training in secretarial skills. If her dreams of becoming a movie star didn't pan out, she would always have something to fall back on.

I can hold a note as long as the Chase National Bank.

After graduating from Bryant High School, she earned twenty-eight dollars a week as a stenographer. She also picked up extra money singing at private parties and nightclubs. She eventually gave up her day job to pursue singing full time. While she was performing between movies at the Brooklyn Paramount Theatre in 1930, Broadway producer Vinton Freedly saw her and engaged her for his next show.

A personally autographed photo of Ethel Merman from *Gypsy* (1961). *Greater Astoria Historical Society.*

The show was George and Ira Gershwin's *Girl Crazy*. When the Gershwins auditioned Merman, they previewed "I Got Rhythm" and "Sam and Delilah" for her, and George graciously said that he'd be happy to change anything she didn't like in them. Slightly shocked, Merman managed to blurt out, "They will do very nicely, Mr. Gershwin"—the first legendary Merman quote.

Merman's clarion voice and hilarious comic timing made her a sensation on opening night, with the audience demanding encores and extra curtain calls. Overnight, the stenographer from Astoria became a musical comedy star. *Girl Crazy* began a string of shows that would stretch through the next four decades, from 1930 to 1971.

Always give them the old fire, even when you feel like a squashed cake of ice.

Broadway's finest composers—including the Gershwins, Cole Porter, Stephen Sondheim, Jule Styne, Jerry Herman and Irving Berlin—did some of their finest work for Merman. Berlin said, "You'd better not write a bad lyric for Merman because people will hear it in the second balcony." Porter called her "La Merman" and said she sounded "like a band going by." Small wonder that audiences adored her too—right up to the standing ovations that greeted her last Broadway performances in *Hello, Dolly!* in 1971.

I can never remember being afraid of an audience. If the audience could do better, they'd be up here on stage, and I'd be out there watching them.

Near the end of her life, Merman wrote:

I don't want to sound pretentious, but in a funny way, I feel I'm the last of a kind. I don't mean that there aren't some girls out there somewhere who are just as talented as I was. But even if they are, where will they find the shows like Girl Crazy, Anything Goes, Annie Get Your Gun, Call Me Madam, *and* Gypsy? *They just don't produce those vehicles anymore.*

Chapter 60

ASTORIA CHARACTERS

THE OCTOGENARIAN ACTIVISTS

By Nancy Ruhling, author of "Astoria Characters," March 10, 2010; reprinted with the kind permission of Nancy Ruhling's AstoriaCharacters.com.

O n the emerald green front door of Stanley and Kathleen Rygo's 1890 cottage, there's a Claddagh knocker whose well-worn brass shows that it's no stranger to visitors.

"It is an honor to have you in my house," says Stanley, as he leads the way through the foyer. He doesn't have to say welcome; the souvenir sign from Ireland—Céad Míle Fáilte—conveys that warm message no less than 100,000 times.

Curiously, it is framed by a Celtic cross and a crisscrossed Christmas-red AIDS ribbon.

Kathleen is slowly climbing the stairs from the basement, and before she appears, the brogue of her birth, a sweet counterpart to Stanley's elegant elocution, trills like a songbird.

Stanley, a spritely eighty-three, and Kathleen, an active eighty, have been married for fifty-seven years, and for the last fifty-five of them, they have lived in this house, which is on the way to Kaufman Astoria Studios and within the sound of the bells of Most Precious Blood Roman Catholic Church. She's an Irish immigrant; his father was English and his mother hailed from Sicily, but he was born in Manhattan and has lived eighty of his eighty-three years in Astoria.

Dwarfed by a brand-new McMansion, the "little green house with the American flag out front," as Kathleen calls it, looks as though it were tossed

Stanley and Kathleen Rygor. *Reprinted with the kind permission of Nany Ruhling.*

into its lot by a Kansas twister. What it lacks in stature, it makes up for in heart and hearth.

Stanley and Kathleen are from the old school; he plays gentleman to her lady. Like a ballroom dancer, he takes the conversational lead, and as he's a trifle hard of hearing, she follows and interprets. It's their habit to read the *New York Times* cover to cover and to serve tea and biscuits to their guests.

"Everyone always asks what the secret to our successful marriage is," says Stanley, whose slightly British accent evokes that of a 1940s stage actor. "We're not exactly that compatible, but we're complimentary. Our interests are different. I'm just average, but Kathleen's got intelligence, she's got an IQ through the roof."

Kathleen rolls her eyes. "He's exaggerating."

The story of how Stanley and Kathleen ended up together is the stuff of classic Hollywood musicals.

In 1944, when he was seventeen, Stanley enlisted in the navy. "It was an easy decision," he says. "The navy uniforms were very attractive to girls. The army uniforms were horrible."

Stanley came home from World War II two and a half years later. Kathleen had just come over from Ireland, and they found true love on a Manhattan dance floor. "The first time I saw her, I thought she was beautiful beyond belief," Stanley says.

A bashful and blushing Kathleen adds, "I thought he was handsome, too."

They married, had five children—their framed photos are on the piano in the living room—and set out to have ordinary lives.

It didn't quite turn out that way.

Stanley threw himself into his career. In six decades, he worked his way up from messenger boy to senior vice president at the Wall Street ad agency

Doremus. Kathleen held down the homefront. In the same six decades, she did everything from sewing school clothes to laying the parquet tile on the living room floor.

One year, Kathleen gave Stanley an Irish button accordion. He taught himself to play so she could dance the Stack of Barley and the Siege of Ennis.

They were pretty much going to go quietly into retirement. Although he wouldn't officially clean out his desk until he turned eighty, Stanley cut back his office time to two days a week when he turned sixty-five. "I could have gone on after eighty," he says, "but I didn't want to break any Guinness world records."

He "was lured into singing" with the choir at Most Precious Blood and started playing his accordion in public. (He has a gig at Dempsey's Pub in the East Village every Tuesday evening and goes to Long Island City to play for the New York City Marathon runners as they hit the halfway point.)

Then it happened. Their son Robert announced that he was gay. Stanley and Kathleen hadn't seen this coming. They were shocked. When Robert, who became ACT UP's spokesperson, told them he had AIDS, they turned themselves into activists, and when he died of the disease, at age forty in 1994, they put his ashes in a blue urn on the piano and continued their gay-rights crusade.

For fifty-seven years, Kathleen and Stanley have been devoted to each other.

"I'm conservative in everything else but gay rights," Stanley says. "I feel strongly about gay rights and marriage equality because I know this is what my son would want."

Kathleen's legs aren't as agile as they used to be, but Stanley still rallies himself for the St. Pat's for All Parade in Sunnyside and the AIDS Walk New York. The 10k AIDS Walk gets harder every year, he says, which is why he diligently trains. "I have to keep it up," he says, "because I raise a lot of money."

Recently, he walked the three miles to and from Astoria Park, where he went around the track eight times, adding two miles to the tally. "I think I overdid it," he says, shifting the pumpkin-orange AIDS Walk baseball cap on his head.

As for Kathleen, she's keeping busy, too. As did her mother and her grandmother before her, she's knitting traditional Irish sweaters for her yet-to-be-born great-grandchildren.

Stanley and Kathleen dream of Ireland, but if God doesn't see fit to let them get there again, their beautiful memories will sustain them.

Chapter 61

DEAN OF THE QUEENS COUNTY HISTORIANS

*T*hree days short of his ninety-fourth birthday, Vincent Seyfried passed away in April 2012. His manual typewriter, a relic of the 1940s, is finally stilled after covering thousands of pages with a million letters, our past forever spelled out. Vincent was called the "Dean of the Queens County Historians."

The role of a historian was set long ago. They are the keepers of public conscience and set down the record of the human experience. They helped form religions, cultures and nations. Before we are born, our parents pass on to us, in their genetic code, the history of our species. Modern research can read that code and tell us where our ancestors wandered from the time we left Africa.

But in modern society, for the most part, historians toil in the shadows, their voice like the narrator of a play whose presence is felt but unseen. Yet their role is essential, for they spin the fabric of our lives, weave the tapestry of our narrative and decide who will be forgotten and who is destined for immortality.

Vincent, a retired teacher, had no children and was a widower. It is ironic that, despite the torrent of information he left about others, there is a certain mystery about him. For example, no one has quite figured out just how much he wrote. For nearly sixty years, he produced a steady stream of newspaper indexes, pamphlets of transit lines and community histories of Queens. New titles are being rediscovered all the time. His magnum opus, *The History of the Long Island Rail Road*, is a sprawling seven-volume epic. It remains unfinished; he never got beyond the events of 1916.

Vincent Seyfried. *Western Queens Gazette.*

But of all these topics, Long Island City held particular interest for him. It is our good fortune that he wrote extensively of our community and collected, with keen interest, everything he could find. He had a thousand pictures, wrote at least a dozen volumes and gave a decade of lectures about our community.

Vincent was the primary force behind founding and sustaining the Greater Astoria Historical Society in its early years. He gave lectures nearly every month. What stories he told of our past! Across his pages strode fools and knaves, plain farmers and men of letters. He wrote of railroads that ventured past farms still using oxcarts and magnificent side-wheel steamers that nearly tipped over from excited crowds waiting to disembark for a day of fun in North Beach. His colorful words painted shifty ward healers collecting bets, votes and payoffs. He wrote of births and deaths and marriages of the obscure and highborn. Vincent compiled lists of our cemeteries, schools, churches, trolley lines. He profiled founding families, distinguished people and the notable events of our past with meticulous detail. Few things of note escaped his attention.

When his sight began to fail and he could no longer drive in from his home in Garden City, Vincent retired from active programing. Our grateful board made him "Honorary Mayor of Long Island City," and we named our research library the Vincent Seyfried Research Center, honors he grudgingly accepted. He never asked for or took a penny. "I am a teacher," he would say. "My legacy is my work."

In April 2012, the New York Academy of History at the Herbert Lehman Center of American History at Columbia University awarded its first Herbert H. Lehman Medal to Vincent for distinguished service to the discipline of history. Unfortunately, Vincent passed away a few days later. Thus, he never learned of his acceptance into the first rank of historians.

The academy decided, therefore, to give the Greater Astoria Historical Society his medal. We accepted it and will place it on permanent display. We pledge to our Long Island City community our commitment to continue his work.

Chapter 62

TO BEAR WITNESS

*How do I keep my craft alive in a world that doesn't value it?
I feel like I am the last reporter in the YouTube world.*
—*Marie Colvin*

*A*lthough she was known in every major war zone worldwide, garnering her awards in journalism, and renowned in her adopted home, England, she was almost unknown in her native country. Marie was born in Astoria, Queens, where her mother, Rosemary, grew up and met her father, Bill, a Fordham graduate. The family later moved to Long Island, where her sister and mother remain.

She was an independent and strong-willed young lady. She was a creature of her time, smoking pot with her friends yet displaying her drive and intellect early on. When she was abroad as an exchange student and discovered that she had missed the deadline for college admission, she drove to Yale's New Haven campus with her high school transcripts and college boards—a perfect 1600. She gained admittance.

Bravery is not being afraid to be afraid.

At Yale, she became friends with Bobby Shriver, the son of Sargent Shriver, the founder of the Peace Corps, and attended a class taught by John Hersey and read *Hiroshima*, his magnum opus. After that, she began to write for the *Yale Daily News*. Graduating with a degree in anthropology, she soon was in journalism, first working with UPI. After transfer to their Paris Bureau, she

The Marie Colvin Award honors courageous women reporters who make a difference in the world. It was started to honor the courage and memory of the late Colvin, who was assassinated while on assignment. *Public domain.*

moved to London to work for the *Sunday Times* in 1985. She was appointed a correspondent to their Middle East and then Foreign Affairs desks.

> *Our mission is to speak the truth to power. We send home that first rough draft of history.*

She gained media attention with her interviews of Libya's Muammar Gaddafi and Palestine's Yasser Arafat, to whom she once reportedly said during the Oslo peace accords of 1993, "Just put the pencil down and sign it already!"

> *These are not just numbers. I want to tell the stories. These are people who have no voice.*

Colvin's bylines from Kosovo, Chechnya and Zimbabwe made her a legend among the press corps.

> *What is bravery, and what is bravado? Journalists covering combat shoulder great responsibilities and face difficult choices. Sometimes they pay the ultimate price.*

Marie Colvin was killed in 2012 during the Syrian Civil War.

In an interview with the BBC, her mother described her daughter: "Everywhere she tried to help people. She believed she was a witness to the violence and that she could make a difference by showing the full reality of people in trouble, not just a snapshot."

Lyse Doucet of the BBC summed up the feelings of Colvin's colleagues: "The world will miss her because she was the eyes and ears of so many."

> *Be passionate in what you believe. Do it as thoroughly and honestly and fearlessly as you can.*

Chapter 63

A SPORTSMAN AND A TEACHER

On November 1, 1946, a crowd of 7,090 filed into Maple Leaf Gardens to watch history—the first professional basketball game of what later would become the National Basketball Association. The New York Knickerbockers went on to defeat the Toronto Maple Leafs 68-66. On the court for the Maple Leafs, scoring one point from a free throw, was Astoria's Frank Fucarino.

Frank attended Bryant High School, where he learned the fine points of the game in varsity competition. He went on to play at the college level while attending Long Island University from 1939 to 1943. After a stint in the U.S. Army Air Corps during World War II, he continued honing his skills in the Peach Basket League, playing for the semi-pro Elizabeth Braves and the Saratoga Indians.

During the NBA's inaugural 1946–47 season, he played twenty-eight out of sixty games for the Maple Leafs, averaging just 5 points a game, with .268 field goal and .567 free throw percentages—not bad for a time before 3 pointers and the time clock. But by today's standards, the games were low-scoring affairs.

At this point in his life, his scrapbook reveals a midlife change. Fucarino, a professional basketball player, returned home to earn his teaching credentials at Columbia University. He applied and was accepted as a public school teacher in Hightstown, New Jersey, in 1953. Frank was notified, as was customary for that time, by a telegram. However, it took an act by the

From Frank Fucarino's teacher album. *Greater Astoria Historical Society.*

borough's council to approve his contract. Both documents are dutifully tucked away on the leaves of his scrapbook.

The book was a narrative of his early years as a teacher: photographs of him and students in classroom vignettes, student valentines and artwork—the stuff familiar to anyone who has taught young people. A scan of the online newspapers from the time mentions him coaching track meets and advancing into administration as a middle school principal.

But nothing reveals the essence of a person's character as much as a firsthand account of someone who can paint a personal sketch from life. We are fortunate that one of his students wrote a moving essay (excerpted here) for a local New Jersey paper years after graduation and, from the perspective of a mature adult, could look back at his high school experience:

> *Once in a while,* [there is] *that rare teacher, who made you believe in yourself and* [help you] *start to understand what you are all about. Just such a teacher was my sixth-grade teacher Frank Fucarino.*
>
> *Mr. F. showed me many of the proper ways, to not only behave, but the responsibility that I would begin to carry for myself and others.*
>
> *I don't know if Mr. F. is even still alive, but thanks to him,* [he] *started the true ball rolling towards young manhood. Yes, there would be many valleys and peaks to conquer, and many mistakes along the way, but his insight and his caring gave me some much needed lessons.*

Frank Fucarino—veteran, sportsman, teacher, mentor, Astorian—retired to his Astoria home, where he passed away in 2012 at age ninety-two.

Chapter 64

THE BEST FIRST BASEMAN

O n July 20, 1944, the *Long Island Star* sports section featured a photograph with the caption "Big Hitters in Kiwanis League." Among the smiling lads was sixteen-year-old Eddie Ford, who played with the 34th Avenue Varsity in the NYS Kiwanis League. Ford did not go to Bryant High School but Manhattan Aviation to perfect his developing skills. He was nicknamed "Whitey" for his blond hair.

Years later, when asked about his favorite game, he said, "Pitching the Maspeth Ramblers to a 16–11 victory over the Astoria Indians."

His career spanned sixteen years as a Major League Baseball pitcher with the New York Yankees. He was a ten-time All-Star and six-time World Series champion, earning the respect of friend and foe alike. His fellow team members called him the "Chairman of the Board."

In 1958, the *Star* again profiled Ford. "I've got to say this is the best season I've ever had….Everything is going just right for me," said the talented lefthander after pitching an 8–0 victory as part of a doubleheader sweep of the Kansas City Athletics.

In 1961, he won both the Cy Young and the World Series Most Valuable Player Awards. Ford led the American League in wins three times and in earned run average twice. He is the Yankees' franchise leader in career wins, shutouts, innings pitched and games started by a pitcher.

Casey Stengel, proud of Ford's record, boasted, "That man is the best man in the league when he's got it, and he is a lot better than most when he's not quite right too."

After Ford earned twenty-seven victories during the 1961 campaign, in 1962, the Yankees agreed to a $60,000 contract—peanuts by today's terms, but it was also the salary for the mayor of New York City at that time.

Ford had a little help along the way to compiling the highest winning percentage (.690) of any pitcher in the twentieth century: he later admitted to having a unique ring made for scuffing. Likewise, in his co-written biography, *Slick*, he confesses to doctoring baseballs.

He was inducted into the Baseball Hall of Fame in 1974.

Ford moved to Long Island but never forgot his Astoria roots. Jimmy Young ran a bar on 34th Avenue where Whitey, Mickey Mantle and fellow teammates celebrated victories. So when Ford heard the Greater Astoria Historical Society was writing a book on Long Island City, he called, pledging an autographed picture for inclusion.

Whitey Ford. *Greater Astoria Historical Society.*

And Astoria never forgot him either. A baseball field in Astoria was recently renamed Whitey Ford Field. In about 2010, an older man showed up at the historical society. He mentioned that he had played ball with young Ford before getting drafted to fight in World War II. When he got out, friends told him that Ford was a pitcher. He scoffed, "Pitcher? Don't kid me!

"That kid was the best first baseman I ever saw!"

Chapter 65

THE MAYOR

These stories were shared with the Greater Astoria Historical Society by Frank Carrado, the last "mayor" of Long Island City.

Frankie, or, with some friends, Butch, was a timeless fixture in Long Island City, a bit like PS1, the courthouse and the LIC Post Office. Like them, he was a local institution. Unlike them, however, he had a chair reserved for his use at the local precinct.

Other mayors and elected officials would come and go, policies announced and replaced. The city churned as months and years spun by—but the mayor was there, camera in hand, ready to greet equally both celebrity and the guy on the street. Everyone knew Frankie and wanted to take a picture with him. He had a stack of those photos, and among his friends, he would go through the list, ensuring that each person was appropriately listed by name. He said that when he died, he wanted them to be there to pay their last respects, if only as a photo.

The Mayor was a direct link to Long Island City's legendary past—he was born when many were still around fondly recalling the real Mayor Gleason, the ferry to "the City" and the mighty Pennsylvania Railroad. The only boy among sisters, his first "job" was helping a friend coal heaving from the rail cars parked just over a fence from his friend's backyard. His gang shoveled it down a homemade ramp into piles of three or four feet and peddled it around the neighborhood for a few pennies a sack. It kept food on the table.

Frank Carrado. *Greater Astoria Historical Society.*

And there was the affair of everyone in the community getting new footwear after shoeboxes regularly "fell off" freight trains—that is, until the yardmasters got wise and consigned future shipments for right or left feet only.

Frankie, son of Italian immigrants, would tell stories of guys he drove around the neighborhood and through Brooklyn "running numbers" and selling fireworks and the fates of guys who used pinball machines without permission. He showed pictures of underground rooms that few knew filled with heavens knows what.

He recounted an uneventful evening when he was a night watchman for a Newtown Creek warehouse, and a limo showed up in the wee hours of the night. A well-dressed gentleman he knew stepped out and gave him a large bill and said to use it to buy himself a very long lunch. He was a regular at prizefights.

Frankie also told of reports from home about his father, who was gravely ill, and getting him pulled from the front lines during the Korean War to come home. His father pulled through. In Frankie's absence, his unit was attacked and all but annihilated by North Koreans.

Frankie was both a good husband and a good father. He lived to see his grandchildren. But when his wife died, his world changed. He bought a camera and devoted his life to his community, taking hundreds of pictures forever, freezing for posterity the transition of his world to our future.

In 2019, Frankie passed from us. His chair at the precinct awaits his return.

Chapter 66

BRIDGE OF IMAGINATION

*G*reater Long Island City, the legendary birthplace of inventive skill and imagination, has a roster of exceptional examples within the world of industry and creative arts. The latter boasts New York City's most incredible listings of galleries and ateliers outside Manhattan. In addition, our community's array of notable sculptures is on the must-see list of both cognoscenti and amateur devotees from around the world: Noguchi Museum, Sculpture Center, Socrates Sculpture Park and the monuments of Athens Square.

On another level, we are also the place of pilgrimage for those who create art. In Long Island City, we can boast one of the world's great art forges, the Modern Art Foundry. Its works span the globe as the legacy of three generations of the Spring family. Its location, in the former stables of the Steinway Mansion, is most apt. As the Steinways were able to provide the means to bring forth the creative dreams of artists in music, the Spring family shepherds sculptors across the Bridge of Imagination in the often-convoluted process that evolves *idea* into *form*.

The firm's newsletter reflects on their accomplishments: "We strive to provide a sculptor's access to skilled craft persons, tools, machinery, and technology needed. We work on pieces ranging from two inches to 50 feet, from representational to abstract, for the well-known, critically acclaimed artist and the sculptor just enjoying art as an amateur."

Notable local examples of their work (and by no means a complete inventory) include *Hans Christian Andersen* and *Alice in Wonderland* in Central

The logo of Modern Art Foundry. *Used with permission of Modern Art Foundry.*

Park; *George M. Cohan* in Times Square; *Garment Worker* in the Fashion District; *Mayor LaGuardia* at LaGuardia Place; and *Sophocles* here in Astoria's Athens Square Park.

Several years ago, the foundry's newsletter published an interview of then retiring president Bob Spring, the son of founder John Spring and the father of current managers, brother Jeffrey and sister Mary Jo. It gave a rare insider's view on the vital role foundries play within the arts: "The Foundry has a life of its own…able to expand and contract as the times and the market demands. It has been a good life. Artists are great to be around [for] they are full of life and not afraid to express it. In the future, when the artists need us, we will be there."

John Spring passed away on April 27, 2020, at age eighty-seven. The family released a photo. He is smiling.

ABOUT THE AUTHOR

Bob Singleton moved to New York City to both experience life in a great city as well as to seek career opportunities no longer available in the declining rustbelt of his native Pittsburgh.

Bored with routine, he left the corporate world and worked with helping a series of small businesses in the newly minted communities of Soho and Tribeca—which proved far more challenging than anything on Wall Street!

He explored the streets of the greatest city on earth, spending days walking through its neighborhoods. He also discovered his past as a direct descendant of the city's founders who played a role in helping define freedoms that made our city the place that welcomed people from around the globe.

Bob is currently the executive director of the Greater Astoria Historical Society.

The Greater Astoria Historical Society, founded in 1985, is the place to learn about Long Island City and its neighborhoods. Through education programs, exhibitions, special events and its collections, it offers a chance to connect with the heritage of Queens. It focuses on the neighborhoods of the independent city of Long Island City (1870–98): Steinway, Astoria Village, Ravenswood, Dutch Kills, Hunters Point, Sunnyside and Blissville.

Visit us at
www.historypress.com

www.ingramcontent.com/pod-product-compliance
Lightning Source LLC
Chambersburg PA
CBHW060339100426
42812CB00003B/1057